Communications
from the Other Side

Communications from the Other Side

Death is Not the End of Life, Love, or Relationships

Anthony Quinata

4th Dimension Press ■ Virginia Beach ■ Virginia

This book is lovingly dedicated to the late Jasmine Mariz and Natalie Smith–Blakeslee. Until we meet again on the Other Side.

And to Camille Massing, who never stopped believing in me—even when I stopped believing in myself.

Contents

Acknowledgments

It's been said that God watches over children and fools. I'm living proof of the latter.

It's also been said that no one writes a book alone. This book is proof of that as well.

First of all, I want to thank Jasmine Mariz for inspiring me to write this book from the Other Side. I know that time doesn't exist in Heaven, but did you really have to wake me up at 3:30 in the morning?

To my father Antonio: I'm happy that, from the Other Side, you finally "get" me.

To my mother Rosalia: Thank you for teaching your children how to live, how to laugh, and finally, how to die. I'm so happy you and Dad are back together again in Heaven.

To my aunt Sue Salas: Thank you for scaring me half to death with your ghost stories. Of course, neither of us knew that you were laying the foundation for my life's work every time you made me wet my pants!

To my sisters and brothers—Meridith, Nadine, Eddie, and Steve Quinata; to Camille and Steve Massing, and to Cheryl Vidakovich: Thank you for your love, for believing in me and in the work I've been doing, and for supporting me on my journey, both as a medium and now as an author.

To Mike and Jennifer Gilbert: Your prayers for me have been invaluable.

To Cheryl Korkos: When you told me that my "thing" was talking to dead people, you set my world on its ear. I couldn't be more grateful.

To Lauren Wilson: Your belief in me touched my life in ways you'll never know.

To April Palmer: You kept insisting I was more "psychic" than I cared to admit and that I needed to be more patient. You were right on both counts! Thank you.

To all of you who were a part of the fun while investigating hauntings with me: I miss you! We share a lot of great memories, good times, and laughter.

To Laura Rodefer: Thank you for all of your support, your acceptance, and your love of who I am.

To Deb Guinther: Thank you for providing me a "home base" out of Cornerstone Books.

To Stacy Tonelli: Your story is as beautiful as you are. Thank you for allowing me to share it.

To Joey and Sue Moffat: Thanks for all of the Guamanian barbecues at your home and for your friendship.

To Pam Keyser: Thank you for all of your love, help, support, encouragement, and grammar tips. You've been an invaluable friend to me.

To the souls who trusted me enough to bring their loved ones to me: I hope I've served you well.

To Donna Lacey, Patty, Diane Padilla, Sheryl Wagoner-Dunn, Matt Uney, Tamela Burkhe, Laura Rodefer, Tom Bendure, Jim, Deb Guinther, Gina Alianello, Cheryl Vidakovich, Greg A. Raymer, and Linda Clinger: Thank you for sharing your stories with me and for allowing me to share them with others. The healing your stories bring and the effect it has on others will be made known to you, I'm sure, when you reach the Other Side.

To Josie Varga: Without you, this book wouldn't have seen the light of day. Thank you for opening the door for me, my friend.

To Cassie McQuagge and Jennie Taylor Martin of 4th Dimension Press and my editor Stephanie Pope: Thank you for believing that I had a story worth telling and for having the patience to let me tell it.

To everyone at the A.R.E. and 4th Dimension Press: Thank you for doing the important work you're doing and for allowing me to be a small part of it.

To all of you: It doesn't seem to be enough just to say "I love you," but I do love you. And I celebrate all of you every day in my prayers.

Perhaps they are not stars, but rather openings in Heaven where the love of our lost ones pours through and shines down upon us to let us know they are happy.

Eskimo Proverb

Foreword

By Josie Varga

I feel there are two people inside me—me and my intuition. If I go along against her, she'll screw me every time, and if I follow her, we get along quite nicely.

Kim Basinger

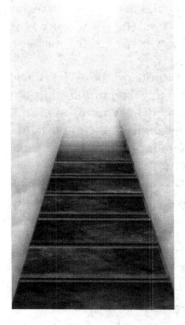

When I came across the above quote, I couldn't help but smile and think of Anthony Quinata. While it is true that Anthony is a very remarkable and talented psychic medium, he didn't accept his gift without a fight. In fact, as he candidly and honestly admits in this book, he did so kicking and screaming. Luckily for all of us, however, he eventually caved in and answered his calling.

The truth is, though, that we all have psychic abilities. We all have the ability to tap into the vast knowledge available to us via our intuition. Being psychic is not some voodoo science. It is a part of all of us. But if you're wondering what sets someone like Anthony apart, it is the complete level of trust that he places in that little intuitive voice inside of his head. Over the years as his abilities have gotten stronger, he has learned to place complete trust in the information that he receives from spirit. Hence the stronger that trust is, the stronger the bond between the here and the hereafter.

Although Anthony recognized his gift as a young boy, he wasn't forced to acknowledge it publicly until years later when his friend Sarah was killed in a tragic car accident. On his way to the memorial service, he spoke out loud to his deceased friend saying, "Sarah, I just want to tell you how sorry I am about what happened to you. I'm still having a hard time accepting it. I love you; I loved our friendship, and I'm going to miss you terribly."

Suddenly, Anthony was aware of his friend's spirit and clearly heard her say telepathically, "I loved our friendship, too. Thank you for being who you are. I'll miss you, too. By the way, tell my family I'm okay!" He admits that he didn't know what to make of it. His initial reaction was to question and doubt what he had experienced, but in his heart of hearts he knew it really was his friend. Since he was new to this work then, he wasn't sure how her family would respond and so he never relayed the message. Nonetheless, his life was forever changed.

I met Anthony when I was working on my book *Visits from Heaven*, which contains evidential afterlife communication accounts from around the globe. I wanted to write a book that would help people understand that they will see their loved ones again, and a mutual friend, the late Natalie Smith–Blakeslee, suggested that I contact Anthony. We became fast friends.

Sometimes people are put in our path for a reason, and I know Anthony is one such person. As I said earlier, he is an incredibly gifted psychic medium. He has brought through many of my deceased relatives and friends with undeniable validations. Time and time again, I continue to be awestruck by the ease with which he connects to the Other Side. He has brought through messages while sipping his coffee at Starbucks and even doing his laundry at home.

But besides the incredible readings, Anthony has helped me to understand that we do not choose to be contacted by our loved ones; we are "chosen." As you read the amazing accounts in this heartwarming book and get acquainted with the Anthony that I've been so blessed to know, I hope you, too, will come to the realization that life never ends and love never dies.

I think Anthony says it perfectly when he writes, "I'm sometimes asked why people who have passed away, would want to communicate with those they have left behind in the first place. It's been my experience that there are a couple of reasons.

"The first one is love. Their physical bodies have died, but their love for us hasn't. They see our pain and want us to understand that while we're no longer connected physically, they are still connected to us emotionally. The second reason is that they can now see the bigger picture in a way we cannot, and they want to help us understand that there's a reason for everything that happens here on this physical plane."

Thank you, Anthony, for all you do to help us see the bigger picture.

Josie Varga
Author of *Visits from Heaven* and *Visits to Heaven*
www.josievarga.com

Preface

With Donna Lacey

I used to do readings out of an office that I shared with a therapist in a complex I swore was designed by an architect while he was on an acid trip. The buildings were put together like a maze, and it took me a long time to learn how to navigate my way from the parking lot to our office. For that reason I would tell people who were coming to see me for a reading to call me from the parking lot, and I'd come out and get them.

I'll never forget the day I went out to meet Donna. When I saw her, the stress on her face literally had me worried about her. Her daughter, on the other hand, was smiling. I could tell that for her, this was going to be an adventure.

Just like everyone else who comes to me for a reading, I didn't know whom Donna and her daughter were hoping to reconnect with, and I didn't want to know. Not that they were going to tell me anyway. In fact, they both agreed that no matter what I said, they were going to say as little as possible to me anyway.

With that, I'll let her tell you her story, in her own words:

* * *

Neither my ex-husband George nor I were brought up to believe that life continued after death. We were raised in a very strict religion from childhood and were taught to believe that Armageddon is due to happen in our lifetime. Fire would rain down from Heaven and all the nonbelievers and those who are weak of faith would be destroyed.

The good news for those who survive is that they go on to rebuild the earth into a paradise. We believed that once people die, they remain dead until God decides to bring them back in the resurrection on earth after Armageddon. Should he choose not to resurrect you, you're just gone for good. It would be as though you had never existed.

I can't express the immense amount of pressure we felt from trying to live up to the standards of this religion. It was as though all our efforts to be strong, spiritual people never seemed to be quite good enough. The result was that it broke our spirit and trust in a God who is supposed to be loving and merciful.

For some reason, I was able to last longer than George. He gave into his insecurities within the first year of our marriage. The pressure was so great that it broke him. He couldn't live up to the expectations of the religion, let alone the expectations he put on himself. I stood by him for years, always feeling that I could somehow pull him through and out of his depression. It didn't quite work out.

After our marriage dissolved, we both quit the religion altogether, much to the chagrin of family and friends. His family lost all respect for him. It was very sad. The heavy guilt was still there, but we continued to search for something different on a spiritual level. George was investigating other churches as well as studying anything he could get his hands on regarding religion and spirituality. We would have long conversations about what could be the real truth regarding God. "Does God exist?" and "What do you believe now?" were questions that would lead to countless discussions.

After our divorce, as hard as it was, we settled into our lives. George and I were still very much friends and partners in raising our children. The kids were with me during the week and with their dad on the weekends. By this time George was suffering from acute pancreatitis, was in extreme pain, and had very little energy. He wasn't his usual self as his illness progressed, and it became increasingly more difficult for him to have the kids on the weekends.

While I did the best I could, all of my energy was spent working two jobs to support the lot of us. Between getting the kids to school each morning and working days, nights, and weekends, I was doing well to just drop them off at George's home on Friday afternoon before another shift. Ironically, I had just left them with a man already dead on his feet, while I was nearly falling down with exhaustion myself.

Somewhere towards the end of 2007, a friend of mine introduced me to a television show on the Lifetime Channel called *Lisa Williams—Life among the Dead*. Oh, did it grab my attention! Could it be true? Could this woman have the ability to hear messages from dead loved ones? Wow, I was enthralled! I was able to open up my mind to the idea that maybe, just maybe, we aren't really gone for good when we die. The experiences on the Lisa Williams' show seemed too real and wonderful not to be true.

Then it happened. At the age of thirty–nine, George succumbed to his illness, and we lost him at the end of January 2008. His death was absolutely devastating to me. It seemed my whole world went right with him. We relied on each other for everything. He truly was my closest friend and kept me grounded to this earth. Nothing seemed right in a world without George! How would I ever raise our children without him? I lost every bit of confidence and couldn't imagine trying to go on without him.

When I discovered that Lisa Williams was coming to Denver to do a live show, I immediately bought tickets in hopes of hearing from George. I had to know if he was still alive somewhere! I'd never looked into psychics or mediums outside of her show—especially since it was strictly forbidden by our former religion and since I was still halfway holding on to what I had been taught about this type of thing. As the date of the show approached, I felt increasingly nervous. I would talk out loud to George, just in case he could hear me and tell him that he had to be there for me! I would cry repeatedly and tell him, "I just need to know you are alive!"

During the show, Lisa said she was getting the name George. I tried to get her attention, but the auditorium was full of people in search of loved ones and she passed on me. Then she brought up a clock or a watch stopped at 4:00. At the end of the show she pulled out a list she had made while in her dressing room for people she had to mention for passed loved ones. Well, she said my daughter's name, but by then I felt deflated at not hearing from George, so I didn't think twice about it.

The next morning, I looked at George's watch on my son's dresser. It was stopped at 4:00! I didn't even know it was broken. I decided to try one more time. I took my daughter with me and we drove to the mall where Lisa was doing a book signing. We stood in line after her talk, and all the while I kept talking to George in my head asking him to please let us know if he was okay. When we approached her, I asked, "Did you ever find the George you were looking for last night?" Surprised, she stopped writing in my book and said, "No!" So, I pulled the watch out and showed it to her. She said, "Oh, my God, that's it!" Of course, she doesn't do readings at her book signings, so I just quickly asked her, "Is he okay?" She said, "He went very quickly; yes, he's okay." I couldn't help shaking.

When she looked back down at the paper her assistant had written our names on, she just stopped. "Oh! This is the name I called out for last night (referring to my daughter). The same spelling, too! I never spell this name that way, but there it is!"

After a few hugs we were on our way. My heart and head were pounding. George is okay!

I started visiting Lisa Williams' Web site daily after my friend showed me that Lisa posts messages from those who have passed for their loved ones. I read through them religiously, just in case George might have something, anything, to say to us.

One day, I found a posting in her blog from someone in Denver who sympathized with her regarding her schedule as he, too, was a medium living a hectic pace, helping people reach loved ones. I couldn't believe it. There was another medium right here in Denver!

Was he real? Could he be someone like Lisa? My mind was in a whirl!

I called to set up an appointment. He was kind and understanding on the phone. I didn't give him a clue as to whom I wanted to hear from or needed to contact. He had to leave town for a week to appear on a television program but promised to meet with me as soon as he could after he returned.

Again, I spoke to George the entire week insisting that he'd better show up for this! I arrived for the appointment with my daughter and a load of insecurity and suspicion. I had absolutely zero confidence that this was going to work.

I was determined not to give this man a bit of information he could use to pretend that someone in spirit was there for us. I was immediately taken with how low key and down-to-earth Anthony was. Even though I was high strung and a bundle of nerves, he remained calm and serene. While arranging the chairs for our meeting, he suddenly stopped and asked, "Who is George?" I said, "He's someone we're here to reach."

He laughed and said, "Well . . . okay; he's already here and we haven't even started yet!" Anthony knew his name right off the bat!

Throughout the entire session, true to my intention, I didn't give Anthony any information he could creatively build on. Yet he went on to describe our lives perfectly. Actually, George went on and on about our lives through Anthony. He laughed a lot and talked about the good times, before he got sick. He talked about the sports car he used to drive. He spoke about his illness and the lack of support from his family right up to the end.

George told me about his life on the Other Side. He talked about the place where he was and would remain for a while in order to rest and recuperate and to adjust to his new reality. He asked me to remember the places in the mountains we used to visit. He said that it's a lot like that for him. He told me to just picture him surrounded by lots of trees and a stream, just the way he likes it! He spends a lot of time by that stream thinking, and the sun is always shining. He said he is the happy-go-lucky guy we all used to know.

He told me . . . when we get there . . . we are all accepted for who we are. That was huge for me!

He apologized for leaving us, especially our thirteen-year-old son, who will need him most of all in these tough years to come. He even brought up the little things that our children and I were now doing on a day-to-day basis which confirmed even more that he was really still with us.

He told us he was at the Butterfly Pavilion with us over the past weekend. He even laughed and brought up that when I hear a bird outside, I'll say hello to him because I feel that it's George saying hello to me!

George reminded my daughter of how he had taught her to ride a bike. He told her to keep an eye out for butterflies, because it was her father saying hello. Now, it's amazing to watch my daughter ride her bike up and down the street with butterflies following her!

Anthony also mentioned the watch and asked why it was stopped at 4:00. I couldn't believe he had mentioned it, because I didn't even bring it with me!

I was overwhelmed with relief after our meeting. Just to know he was still alive, not sick nor in pain anymore! He was just fine! Of course, the grief still crept in from time to time. The guilt of how our lives played out and his love for me, even after the divorce, kept haunting me.

A second visit to Anthony did much to heal my wounds. George was right there again to insist that he was still with us and loved us and will always be there to help. He even brought my grandfather with him this time. George and my grandfather, also named George, got along quite well. They had a deep respect for one another. George mentioned him often after my grandfather died, not so many years ago, especially since my grandfather died of pancreatic cancer and our George's condition was very similar. George often thought of my grandfather during his own illness. I think it is wonderful they are together now in the same place.

Then Anthony told me my grandfather wants me to say hello to his wife, "Um, Myrtle, like turtle?" I couldn't believe he [Anthony] said my grandmother's name! There is no way he could just pull a name like "Myrtle" out of the air like that!

This visit proved even further that there really is life after death. No longer will I fear death.

George restored my belief in God, the "Powers that Be," or a "Life Source!" No longer will I live in fear of a God who doesn't accept us for who we are. George's passing simply led to his rebirth into a new life!

Just days before he passed away, George mentioned to me two things he feared. One was that the world would go on as if he had never even been there. The second was that he would be forgotten. My life and my children's lives will certainly never be the same without him, and he knows for sure that he could never, ever be forgotten.

My healing has begun. I go back from time to time to listen to the recordings of the meetings with George through Anthony. I can't speak for the validity of all mediums, but Anthony has more than proven he is the real deal. I know I can never repay him for what he has done for us. This gift is truly priceless.

Donna Lacey

Introduction

I didn't choose to do this work. It chose me.

I'm originally from Guam, a tiny island in the South Pacific. Joey, a friend of mine who is also from Guam, told me, "When you said to me that you talk to dead people for a living, I didn't doubt you for a moment. Do you know why?"

I was actually stunned when he said that. "I don't have a clue," I said. "Why?"

"No one from our culture, who's in his right mind, would ever make such a claim!" he answered.

I hadn't thought about it before, but what he said was true. When someone dies, we say nine days of prayers (referred to as a "novena"). After that comes the burial. Once people are laid to rest, we don't talk about them. It's believed that doing so disturbs their peace.

When I was growing up, being a psychic medium wasn't at the top of the list of things I wanted to do in my life. It wasn't at the bottom of the list either. In fact, it wasn't on the list, period. People from Guam are typically Roman Catholic, so psychics and psychic phenomenon are not topics of conversation in the typical Guamanian household. While my mother did read her daily horoscope, I didn't even hear the word "psychic" until I was nine years old.

So how did I know that I could talk to dead people? This book is the story of my journey. It's a chronicle of my life, dealing with how I went from not talking about people who had passed away to talking to people who had crossed over and what I've learned along the way.

I did not have any formal training as to how to be a "medium." I was taught how to do this work by the souls who inspired their loved ones to contact me for a reading.

I've learned a lot along the way, and I'm still learning from the souls on the Other Side who use me as an instrument to reconnect them with the loved ones they've left behind. In this role, I've been privy to messages of love, hope, and healing.

I used to wonder what happens after we die. I dreaded the idea of never seeing the people I love ever again. I've since learned that what we refer to as "death" is simply a passage from this reality to a life that continues on in another plane of existence and that those we loved and those who loved us do not die. It's my hope that after reading this book, you'll know this too.

The best way to help you understand these lessons is to tell my story and those of some of the people who have come to me for readings over the years. Everyone you're about to meet is a real person who has graciously shared the experience of the reading with me.

I'll be honest, for years I wondered why souls wanted to communicate with their loved ones and whether the readings served any purpose at all. Typically, once the session was over, I didn't hear another word from the person, or people, who had received the reading. Because of this, I didn't think that there was any real benefit from hearing what the souls had to say.

Then I received an email from a producer of the Oprah show who said she wanted to do a television show on mediums and asked if I would I send testimonials from people who had received a reading from me.

I asked around and found people more than willing to write one for me. When I read them, I was stunned to find out the effects that the messages from the souls had had on people.

The letters were powerful and illuminating for me. I decided to share a few of them with the hope that they have the same effect on you. You'll find them under "My Reading with Anthony."

I was brought into this work kicking and screaming. Now I do it with a sense of awe and amazement at the beauty of the souls who do the communicating and of the God who wills it to happen. I'm so overwhelmed by the experience of what I do that I don't feel any need to embellish or exaggerate any of the stories to make a point.

This is as accurate a portrayal of my life as a reluctant medium as I can make it. As my friend Jim used to say, "Believe it . . . or don't."

Blessings,
Anthony
April 2, 2012

Chapter

1

I seriously doubt I would even be doing this work if it weren't for my aunt Sue. Sue isn't from Guam, but from Japan. She is married to my uncle Joe, who is my mother's brother.

It's very common for young men from Guam to sign up for military service. My father was a career Navy man, working on an aircraft carrier, the U.S.S. Yorktown, up until I was ten years old. My uncle was career Army. Both of them served overseas during the Korean and Vietnam wars. My family and my Aunt Sue's family lived in Southern California, so we spent a lot of time at my aunt's home.

One night, when I was eight years old, my aunt told me a Japanese ghost story that frightened the living daylights out of me. It scared me so much that I jumped out of my chair, and to this day I believe I actually had to use my hands to keep my head from hitting the ceiling!

Everyone laughed at me, but after that, I was hooked. Every time I'd spend the night at her house, I'd ask her to tell me another ghost story which usually meant I'd be so afraid that I'd have to change my underwear and lie in bed terrified of the ghost I was sure was going to come for me, either out of the closet or from under the bed.

"Were there really such things as ghosts?" I wondered. The answer to my question came one night when I was watching television with my mother. My sister Meridith and my brother Eddie were both asleep, and after watching an episode of "Batman," I was ready to fall asleep as well. The television set that my mother and I were watching was in the bedroom I shared with Eddie. As soon as the show ended, I asked my mother if she wanted to keep watching television.

My mother asked me if I was ready to go to bed. Since I indicated that I was, she told me to go ahead and turn off the television. As soon as I did, we both heard a very loud, male voice call out my mother's name.

"Rosalia!"

I stood next to the television looking at my mother. We were both wondering the same thing, "Had someone broken into our house?"

"Who are you?" my mother asked.

Once again we heard the same voice say, "Rosalia!"

"What do you want?" my mother asked, clearly afraid.

After that, we heard muttering and what sounded like the front door being slammed shut, followed by the screen door. "Go check the front door and make sure it's locked," my mother told me.

I ran out into the living room and checked the front door. "It's locked!" I called out to my mother.

"Check the screen door!" I opened the front door and let her know that it was locked too.

I don't know how long it took my mother to finally fall asleep, but I fell asleep rather quickly, happy to have had what I thought was my first experience with a real "ghost."

The next day my mother decided we were going to spend the night at my Aunt Sue's house. When my mother told Sue what had happened, my aunt said (of course, I was eavesdropping on their conversation) that someone had been knocking on her back door for three straight hours! Sue told us that she kept asking, "Who is it?" When no one answered and the knocking persisted, she picked up a carving knife, held it up in the air, and said, "Come in!"

No one did, but the knocking on the door continued.

The next day my mother received a call from one of her sisters. Their father was ill and in the hospital. At one point, my mother was told that my grandmother was unconscious and kept muttering, "Rosalia, José," over and over again.

Technically, what happened is what is referred to in parapsychology as a "crisis communication." Typically, crisis communications occur when someone is seriously injured, ill, or dying, and that person telepathically reaches out to someone close to them. Usually the person who is doing this isn't aware that a message is being sent out.

I didn't know about crisis communications when I was eight years old, but what my mother and I heard that night convinced me that ghosts do, indeed, exist, and it was the beginning of what would become an obsession that would last for years.

Chapter

2

When I was ten years old, my father was assigned to duty in Iceland. We were living in Norfolk, Virginia at the time. He went first, and we followed a few months later so that Meridith, Eddie, and I could finish school. While we were still in Virginia, there was a new addition to our family—my sister Nadine.

When we finally arrived in Iceland, one of the things I remember is because it was so cold that when my father saw us, he started crying and his tears literally froze on his face. Still, to this day, I loved living there.

There was a small library on the military base where we lived. I

5

found and read the book *A Gift of Prophecy* written by the psychic Jeanne Dixon. It was my first real introduction to anything "psychic." In her book she wrote that she knew she was "special" because the lines in one of her palms formed a star. I looked at both of my palms—no star. I wasn't a psychic, and I can't tell you how disappointed I was. I was, however, so fascinated by her story that I think I read her book, cover to cover, at least three times.

I saw another book in the "base exchange," which is kind of like a Walmart store for military personnel and their families, entitled *How to Tell Fortunes with Ordinary Playing Cards.* It was on the same shelf as the monthly magazines my mother would buy that had daily horoscope predictions for every sign in the zodiac. All I saw was the cover of the book. I didn't pick it up to look at it because I didn't have the money to buy it, and I didn't think my mother would buy it for me either.

A few days later my mother was reading the predictions for the day in one of her magazines, and I saw a deck of cards that my parents had been using the night before to play poker with their friends. Remembering the book I had seen about telling fortunes with ordinary cards, I asked my mother if she'd like me to tell her fortune for her.

"How are you going to do that?" she wanted to know.

"With these cards," I told her, shuffling the deck.

I don't think she had ever received a "card reading" before, but I am sure that she thought the idea of receiving one from her ten-year-old son was amusing. "Sure," she said, "Tell me my fortune."

As I said before, I didn't look inside of the book, so I really had no idea what I was supposed to do. I hadn't heard of tarot cards and knew nothing about card spreads. What I did do was lay the cards out in three rows of seven. I got the idea from a card trick my father had taught me.

After I laid the cards out, I looked them over and said the first thing that came to mind. "Your father's in the hospital."

"What?" my mother asked. She didn't seem to find what I was doing as funny as she had a moment ago.

"Your father's sick. He's in the hospital."

"How do you know that?" my mother demanded to know. She wasn't taking what I said seriously; she just couldn't believe I had the gall to say what I was saying.

"That's what the cards are telling me," I said. "Your father is sick, and he's in the hospital."

"If my father is in the hospital, I would know about it. One of my sisters would have called and told me." With that she got up and walked away.

I shrugged my shoulders and put the cards back together in the deck. I wondered why she was so upset. It wasn't like I knew what I was doing.

The next day my mother received a phone call from one of her sisters telling her that my grandfather was in the hospital, but not to worry. The doctors said that he was doing fine and would be out soon. After my mother got off of the phone, she asked me, again, how I could possibly have known that my grandfather was in the hospital.

"As I said," I told her, "it's what the cards were telling me." The truth is the cards weren't telling any such thing. I just remember it was a feeling I got when I was looking at them.

My mother was so shaken by what happened that she told our next door neighbor about it. Our neighbor, while stunned because what I "predicted" turned out to be true, apparently found the whole thing funny as well.

"Wow! Are you a psychic, Anthony? Are you a fortune teller?" she asked me, laughing hysterically.

"I'm not a psychic," I thought. "I don't have a star in the palm of my hand."

A week later my mother asked me to tell her fortune again. I got the cards and started laying them out the same way I had done before. This time I didn't finish . . . I stopped when I got a "feeling" from one of the cards. Even today, I remember the card; it was the nine of clubs.

"You're going to break your leg," I said, hesitantly. I remember being afraid to even look up at her.

Her reaction was exactly the same as when I told her that her father was in the hospital. "What are you talking about?"

"You're going to have an accident, and you're going to break your leg," I told her, still not wanting to look at her, so I just continued staring at the cards.

My mother didn't want to hear any more of my nonsense. Once again, without saying a word, she got up and walked away.

A couple of days later my mother had taken my sister Nadine, who was just a few months old, for a checkup. When she came back home, she lifted Nadine out of the car and noticed toys in a neighbor's yard that looked like toys we owned. She kept looking at them wondering if Meridith, or I, had left them in that yard. She kept walking, not paying attention to where she was going and not seeing the ice in front of her on the sidewalk. When she stepped on it and lost her footing, her first instinct was, of course, to make sure Nadine didn't get hurt. She protected Nadine's head and body with her arms, and when she fell, she broke her leg.

She never asked me for another "reading" after that nor did our next door neighbor. The idea that I might actually be a "psychic" never came up again. After all, we were still a good Guamanian family.

Chapter

3

After Iceland, my father was stationed at a naval base in Indiana. It was there that my youngest brother Steve was born.

We lived in a small town, and I went to a small school several miles away. I developed a reputation for being a weirdo interested in psychics, ghosts, and witches. Virtually every day I went to school, I was harassed about it. So much so that one of my eighth grade teachers brought a "test" to class which was designed to determine if someone had ESP. Guess who was the only one assigned to take the test.

According to my teacher, if I answered seven of the ten questions correctly, then it was "possible" that I might actually have extra sensory perception. I don't remember what the questions were, but I do remember surprising everyone, including myself, by answering the first six questions correctly.

I also knew the answer to the seventh question. I could see the answer clearly in my mind's eye. Now I faced a dilemma. Do I answer the question or don't I? I was already feared and hated by much of the school, and most of those people thought of me as a nut case. Like so many kids that age, I wanted more than anything else to just fit in.

I decided that answering the question would only make things worse for me than they already were, so I claimed ignorance. My teacher and classmates all laughed at me. She didn't bother asking the remaining questions. I did get what I wanted though. The harassment I was subjected to started to ease up slowly.

After that, my classmates began welcoming me with open arms. My intense interest in things paranormal gradually began to be replaced by playing baseball and basketball and by joining the track team.

An incident happened later that did keep my interest in ghosts alive though. One day I heard on the news that a female student at Indiana University in Bloomington was murdered the night before. Later that day, Julie, one of my neighbors, asked me if I had heard about what had happened.

I told her I had and she said, "Did you know that she used to live where you live now? She grew up in that house." I didn't know that, and now that I did, I wasn't sure I wanted to know. It just seemed creepy to me.

I told my parents about it and that somehow gave them the idea that going shopping in Bloomington later that day was a good idea! I didn't want to go, so I was alone in the house, reading a book, when I suddenly thought about the girl who was killed the night before. I thought about how she had lived, played, eaten, and slept in the very house I was in. Suddenly, the glass of a small kerosene lamp that hung on the wall between my room and Meridith's room exploded sending glass all over the hallway floor.

I sat there trying to decide whether I should clean up the glass or run screaming out the door. There was another kerosene lamp hanging on the wall between two other bedroom doors that didn't explode, which made me wonder if she had slept in either Meridith's bedroom or mine.

I came to the conclusion that since I was sitting there, it must have been mine. That made me want to pack my clothes and move out, and I probably would have done so if it weren't for the big wet spot on the front of my pants.

When nothing else happened for about an hour afterwards, I decided it was safe to change my pants and sweep the glass up off the floor, saying a prayer for the young university student as I did so.

Chapter

4

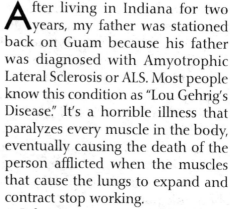

After living in Indiana for two years, my father was stationed back on Guam because his father was diagnosed with Amyotrophic Lateral Sclerosis or ALS. Most people know this condition as "Lou Gehrig's Disease." It's a horrible illness that paralyzes every muscle in the body, eventually causing the death of the person afflicted when the muscles that cause the lungs to expand and contract stop working.

It became an opportunity to become reacquainted with my culture. The Chamoru mindset is based on respect, which extends to those who have died. We also have a great deal of respect for our ancestors, whom we refer to as **taotaomona** (*tao-toe-mo-na*).

We moved into a home that belonged to my mother's parents while we waited for military housing to become available. One of the stories that my mother told us was that my grandfather was out in a field behind the house when he saw a young boy staring at him. My grandfather asked the boy who he was and what he was doing there. The boy vanished. My grandfather believed, until the day he died, that he had seen a taotaomona.

Strange occurrences happened while we lived in that house. For example, it was so hot and humid during the day that I typically took a shower at night. I noticed that when I finished and stepped out of the tub, the air around me was freezing. I started opening the bathroom window after I took a shower; then I began opening it before I took a shower. The result was always the same. Instead of stepping out of the tub into humid, tropical air, I always felt as though I were stepping into a walk-in freezer. My teeth would literally chatter while I was drying myself off. I finally started wrapping my towel around my waist, and I would walk out of the bathroom and into my bedroom to dry off and put clothes on. Then I would walk back into the bathroom to hang my towel back up. When I did, I'd notice that the air was usually warm and humid again.

What I didn't know at the time was that the "chill" I felt is the way my body reacts when I'm in the presence of a spirit. I still get same sort of feeling to this day when I'm in the presence of an apparition.

I didn't say anything to anyone about it, but one night when my family was eating dinner, my brother Eddie, who was ten at the time, innocently asked, "Has anyone noticed anything weird about this house?"

"What do you mean by weird?" I asked him.

"Sometimes at night when I'm falling asleep, I'll hear what sounds like someone running around in the attic," he said.

"I haven't heard that," I responded, "but has anyone noticed that whenever I take a shower I go into my room to dry off?"

"Yeah, I have!" Meridith piped in. "Why do you do that?"

"Because, whenever I'm done taking a shower, the bathroom is freezing!"

"Wow, do you think that this house is haunted?" Meridith asked.

"I don't know but . . . ," I started to say when my father interrupted.

"That's enough of that kind of talk," he said angrily. "You're scaring the babies. Besides, there's no such thing as ghosts." I remember being surprised that my father would even say such a thing considering the fact that I had heard more ghost stories on Guam than anyplace else we had lived.

Did my father really believe that ghosts don't exist? If he didn't, something happened in that house a couple of weeks later that seemed to change his mind. My mother was gone one afternoon to pick up Eddie from school, and when she returned twenty minutes later, my father was sitting on the porch waiting for her with nothing on but his underwear and a T-shirt.

My grandparent's home was at the end of a secluded dirt road. Even so, my mother was so shocked to see my father like that she asked, "What are you doing outside in your underwear? What if someone sees you like that?"

My father answered her question by saying, "Don't ever leave me alone in this house again."

"Why, what happened?" my mother asked, concerned because my father looked so scared.

"This house is weird," was all my father would say. He refused to say anything more.

It wasn't until more than thirty years later when he told my sisters what had happened that day. "I was taking a nap in the living room while your mother went to pick up Eddie from school. Suddenly, I woke up when I heard what sounded like someone running back and forth in the attic! I was so scared I sat outside waiting for Mom."

There were four other houses on the road that led to our home. The first house belonged to an uncle who was never there. I was told he was always traveling. One night I was walking home when I noticed five men, sitting on their haunches, talking quietly, almost as though they were whispering. I was excited because I'd finally have a chance to meet my elusive uncle.

I walked up to them, waving, and saying, "Hi, Uncle! When did you get back?" All of a sudden, all of the men stopped talking and simply stared at me. It wasn't exactly the response I was expecting, and I stood there looking back at them.

When I finally got the idea that I wasn't welcome, I backed up, not taking my eyes off of them, nor they me, until I felt the dirt and gravel of the road under my flip flops. I walked home wondering what was up with my uncle. Yeah, he didn't know me, but I thought he would have been friendlier.

I got home and asked my mother, "When did uncle get back?" She asked me which uncle I was referring to. "The one who lives in the first house," I told her. She told me that he still hadn't come back.

I told her about the men I saw and what had happened when I talked to them." Where did you see them," she asked, looking more concerned than I thought was necessary.

"Near the banyan (breadfruit) tree in front of his house," I said, nonchalantly, not thinking anything about it.

"Were you afraid?" she asked.

"No, I just thought he'd be more excited to see me. But if it wasn't him . . . "

"I think you saw the taotaomona," my mother said, quietly. She said this because the people of Guam believe that our ancestors live in the roots of the banyan tree, which rise above the ground, and form what looks like a hut. I didn't bother telling my father what I saw. After all, didn't he just tell us that ghosts didn't exist?

I didn't think much more afterwards about what had happened that night; although any night that I walked by my uncle's house, there could have been a five-piece band playing John Philip Sousa songs and I still would have made sure I didn't look in the direction of that banyan tree!

When "base housing" finally became available for us, my parents rented my grandparent's house to a "stateside" couple with three kids. I don't remember much about them except that the husband, Rick, talked about running for a seat in the Guam Senate, and his wife, Jeanne, was a columnist for the local newspaper.

A couple of months after we moved out and they moved in, my mother received a call from Jeanne asking that the shed on the side of the house be taken down. My mother told her that my cousin Roque and I would be happy to do it (not that she had asked either one of us).

While Roque and I were taking the shed apart, my mother and Jeanne talked through the kitchen window. I took a short break to ask Jeanne for a couple of glasses of water. As Jeanne was getting the water, she hesitantly said to my mother, "Rose, may I ask you and Anthony a question? Has anything strange ever happen while you lived in this house?"

She had my interest now, and even though she handed me two glasses of water through the kitchen window, I wasn't going anywhere!

My mother answered her question with a question. "What do you mean?"

"Well . . . " Jeanne continued. I could tell she was struggling with whether or not she even wanted to tell us what she was about to say. " . . . every once in a while we'll leave and when we come back home, all of the lights will be turned on in the house, the burners in the stove are turned on, and the water in faucets will be running . . . and this happens in the middle of the afternoon! This kept happening and we thought the kids were leaving everything on. So Rick and I would go through the entire house before we'd leave and make sure everything was off. When we'd come back, everything was turned on again!"

My mother and I looked at each other not knowing what to say. Finally my mother said to Jeanne, "Those things didn't happen when we lived here."

The fact that we didn't laugh at her or disbelieve what she was saying seemed to encourage Jeanne to tell us more. "Just the other night I was falling asleep and I heard what sounded like our vacuum cleaner in the living room! So I got up wondering why one of my kids was running the vacuum in the middle of the night. I put my robe on, and as soon as I put my hand on the doorknob, the sound stopped. I opened the door, walked into the living room, and there in the middle of the floor was our vacuum plugged into the wall!"

I was stunned. Nothing like that had ever happened while we lived there, though I thought it would have been exciting if it had. For me it would have proven ghosts do exist no matter what my father said.

"What did you do?" I asked. By this time, Roque had become tired of waiting for me to bring him his glass of water and was walking up to where my mother and I were standing. I handed him his glass and whispered, "Stay here. You've got to hear this!" even though I knew that he had not only a healthy respect for the dead and the taotaomona, but also an even healthier fear of them as well.

"I unplugged the vacuum, wrapped the cord around the handle, and put the vacuum back in the closet. I checked in on the kids, and they were all fast asleep."

I told Roque what Jeanne had just said to my mother and me about the vacuum. Just as I suspected he would, he gulped down his water, handed his glass to Jeanne, and walked back to what remained of the shed. I couldn't help but smile as I watched him walk away as fast as he could trying not to be obvious about it. I knew he wanted to finish taking down the shed, all by himself if he had to, so that he could get home and as far away from my grandparent's house as fast as possible.

When I turned back around, Jeanne continued her story. "I went back to my bedroom and was just about to fall asleep when I heard the vacuum again! So I got up, put my robe on, and as soon as I touched the doorknob, the noise stopped. I walked out into the living room, and there was the vacuum, plugged into the wall, in the middle of the floor!"

I wanted to hear if anything else happened in the house, but I started to feel guilty about leaving Roque all alone to work on the shed. When we finished, my mother and I got in our car and went home. We didn't say a word to each other about what Jeanne had told us, but my interest in ghosts had just been re-kindled, and it would soon burst into a full blown obsession.

Tropical storms and typhoons are a part of life on Guam, and every once in a while a storm would approach the island that would have people boarding up their windows, or if you lived in military housing, putting up metal storm shutters. Once, when just such a storm was coming, a few friends of mine and I de-cided to have a "storm shutter party." We went to each other's home and put shutters in the windows.

The last house we did was for a girl named Patty. A straight "A" student, Patty was not known for making stories up to get atten-tion, but what happened that day certainly got mine. After we had finished putting up the shutters on the windows of Patty's home, she told us that she had made sandwiches for us to eat and to help ourselves while she went upstairs to take a shower.

Twenty minutes later we were all standing in the kitchen, the sandwiches gone, talking, waiting for Patty to come back down-stairs. Suddenly, we heard a blood curdling scream coming from upstairs. We found Patty in her room, trembling and crying un-controllably.

When she finally calmed down enough to talk to us, we asked her what had happened. She told us that after she took a shower, she was in her room standing in front of the mirror brushing her hair. She could see her bedroom window and how the shutter enabled her to see the reflection of her room in the window. Then she noticed something that scared the living daylights out of her.

"I was brushing my hair when I noticed a movement out of the corner of my eye. I looked in the mirror, and I could see a young girl with long blonde hair, wearing a white T-shirt and blue jeans reflected in the window. She looked as though she was looking directly at me, and she had her right hand in the air, above her head, as though she were holding something in her hand."

"What was she holding?" we asked her. "Was it a knife?"

"I don't know," Patty said. "Her hand was cut off by the edge of the window. I turned around to look for her, but there was nobody there. When I looked back in the window, she was walking towards me and her hand was coming down, almost as if she was holding a knife and was going to stab me. That's when I started screaming."

Several months later I asked Patty about that day and if she now believed in ghosts because of what she saw. "Honestly, Anthony," she told me. "I just don't know. Now I think it was just all my imagination, that's all." That's all she would say about what had happened from that day forward.

Even though I didn't experience what she saw personally, I knew she had seen a ghost. When I found her in her room, she was too terrified for it to be just her imagination. She had seen a ghost. I might have seen taotaomona, but to me, they weren't really ghosts. They were my ancestors, guardians of the island.

In my mind, I could explain the taotaomona. I wanted to see, and experience, something I couldn't explain. I wanted to see something like what Patty saw. I wanted to see a "real" ghost.

Chapter

5

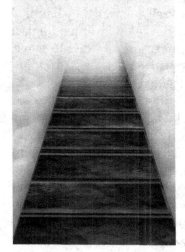

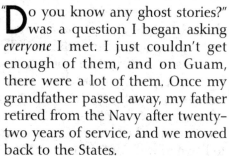

"**D**o you know any ghost stories?" was a question I began asking *everyone* I met. I just couldn't get enough of them, and on Guam, there were a lot of them. Once my grandfather passed away, my father retired from the Navy after twenty-two years of service, and we moved back to the States.

While I was on Guam, it seemed like most of the people who lived there, including those who weren't native to the island, took the existence of ghosts as a matter of fact. Perhaps it's because there isn't a square inch of the island that hasn't been soaked in blood from all the wars fought on the island, starting with the Spanish–Chamoru war fought between 1671 and 1695 and ending so far with the battles between the Japanese and American armed forces for control of the island during World War II.

When we moved back to the States, though, whenever I asked if anyone knew of any haunted houses or had experienced anything supernatural, I typically received a look that said, "Do you really believe in ghosts?" It reminded me of the time I grew up in Indiana, so I became more careful of whom I asked.

I had a wander lust in my 20s, so I moved around a lot. Around 1983, I lived in Salt Lake City for about seven months. I met a couple of women, Karma and Peggy, who shared a trailer home. As I got to know them better, I asked, "Do you know of any true ghost stories or haunted houses?"

"We think our trailer is haunted," Karma told me.

"Why's that?" I asked her.

"Both of us feel like there's a man watching us sometimes. We haven't seen him. We just feel someone staring at us."

It wasn't the kind of exciting story I was hoping for so I let it drop. A couple of weeks later, I had my first experience communicating with someone who had died in that same trailer.

I was at a party that got a little out of hand, and the police were brought in to quiet things down. Well, the way they handled the situation got way out of hand, and I decided I wanted no part of what seemed to be coming down next and decided to leave. The two guys I came to the party with had similar ideas, deciding to leave as well. Unfortunately, they decided to leave without me.

I didn't know who else to call, so I phoned Karma and asked her if she would come and get me. She agreed even though she lived several miles out of Salt Lake City in a town named West Jordan. Peggy was with her when she picked me up, and we went back to their trailer.

I was sitting on the floor talking to them. They were seated at the kitchen table when I saw a man standing behind Karma in the hallway leading to their bedrooms. He was Caucasian, wearing a plaid shirt and khaki pants. I thought it was curious that he was barefooted. I knew that neither of the girls could see him, because they weren't saying anything.

I can't remember what we were talking about, but whatever it was, I stopped the conversation completely when I asked them, "Didn't you tell me that your home is haunted?"

"Well, we think it is," Karma said. "It always feels as though a man is watching us. Why?"

"Well, you're going to think I'm crazy, but I can see a man standing in your hallway!"

They both looked at the hallway, and then looked back at me. "Well," I thought to myself, "that confirms it. Someone either slipped something into my drink at the party, or I'm actually seeing a ghost." I went with the idea of seeing a ghost. Because without him actually speaking to me, I knew what he wanted me to say.

"He wants me to tell you that he's sorry he scares you when he opens the door to the master bedroom as you two are taking a shower."

When I said that, both of them screamed. They then told me that the only bathroom in the trailer is in the master bedroom and that's usually where they feel like they're being watched. In addition to this, since there's no door to the bathroom, they close the bedroom door for privacy when they take a shower. Once it's closed, it's really difficult to open, yet they constantly step out of the shower and find the door wide open.

Karma told me that one time she was drying her hair when she saw the door open and on the other side was her six-year-old grandson. "There's no way he can open that door once it's closed."

I asked them to show me, and we all walked to the bedroom. The door was open and Karma shut it. I turned the door knob and pushed. The door barely moved. I pushed again. It gave a little more, but didn't open. Finally, I put my shoulder against the door, pushed, and the door opened. "I'm surprised either of you can even open this door once it's shut," I told them.

Later that night I was sleeping on the couch when I woke up

suddenly. I couldn't breathe, and I heard what sounded like air bubbles rushing past my ears, as though I was underwater. For a moment I thought I was under water. "Oh my God, I'm drowning!"

I opened my eyes, looked around, and remembered where I was. I pushed against the top of the couch with my left hand and grabbed the bottom of the couch with my right. I landed on the floor, and the feeling of being underwater was gone. I lay back down on the couch knowing that there was one more message I was supposed to deliver.

The next morning when Karma was in the kitchen making breakfast, I asked her, "Was this area ever underwater?"

"Oh yeah, in fact, it's named after the Jordan River," she told me.

"Did anyone ever drown here?"

"A lot of people," she told me. "That's why the river was drained. Why?"

"I think I know why that guy is hanging around your trailer." I explained what happened to me in the middle of the night. "I think he drowned in the spot where your couch is. If I'm right, you shouldn't have any more problems feeling like you're being watched."

I didn't see Karma again for another three weeks, and when I did, I asked her if anything strange had happened in her home after that night. "You know, now that you mention it, we haven't had anything at all happen since then. Not even the door opening, and that's what scared us the most!"

When I share that story, I'm often asked if that's when I realized I was a psychic medium. The answer is "no." If you would have asked me at the time, I wouldn't have been able to tell you what a medium was or did. I didn't know, and I didn't care either.

Chapter

6

I left Salt Lake City and moved back to Southern California. I was driving past a sign that I had seen a number of times but hadn't paid attention to. It had the profile of a Native American with a headdress of eagle feathers. Above the profile was the word, "Psychic."

Below were the words, "Tarot and Palm Readings." Below that was written, "Past, Present, and Future."

It was the word, "Future," that caught my attention. "If that so-called psychic could really predict the future," I thought, "why does she live in that shack?"

With that thought, the seed of my skepticism—okay, my cynicism about psychics—was planted. I'm not sure why, but I soon began to think that most, if not all of them, were charlatans. I used to joke that if someone really was psychic, as soon as I sat down in front of him, he'd know I was about to write him a bad check and that he'd be calling the police to come and arrest me.

After living in Southern California, I moved to the San Francisco Bay area and from there to Denver, Colorado. It was after I moved to Denver in 1988 that I saw a show on television about a group of people who investigated reports of ghosts and hauntings.

"Wow!" I thought to myself. "Now that looks like fun!" And I wanted to get in on it. Based on what I had seen on the show, I went out and bought a camera, and I was off to the races! Of course, I had no idea what I was doing, but that sort of thing had never stopped me before. Basically, my "investigations" consisted of going through cemeteries during the day and trespassing in them at night. If a building was supposedly haunted, I found an excuse to get inside and take pictures. Occasionally, someone would actually let me in his home to do an "investigation."

I read every book I could get my hands on about investigating the paranormal. One of the books I perused was Harold Sherman's *The Dead Are Alive*. The subtitle of the book was *They Can and Do Communicate with You!*

I read the book with a great deal of skepticism. It was about experiments being done in which voices of those who had passed away were being recorded by researchers around the world. I found out in another book that this is referred to as Electronic Voice Phenomenon or EVP for short.

Even though I was skeptical, I was excited by the possibility that not only would I be able to hear the voices of those who have died, but that I could also do it from the comfort, and privacy, of my own home! Sherman wrote that in order to do this, I needed to buy a reel-to-reel tape recorder with the capability to record at various speeds. "Okay," I thought, "I haven't seen a reel-to-reel recorder since my father had bought one when I was five years old, but if that's what I have to do . . . " I couldn't wait to get started, and I was quickly able to find a store that actually sold refurbished reel-to-reel recorders. I bought one for $120 (in 1989 dollars).

After several attempts at capturing voices from beyond, I just wasn't getting the results Sherman wrote about, so I looked for other books on the subject. Imagine my surprise when I found out that people were getting results with ordinary, inexpensive cassette recorders!

I went out and bought a cassette recorder and conducted several more experiments with no success. I just couldn't understand what I was doing wrong. I tried buying and using different microphones. One night I made a recording, and the next morning I was excited to hear heavy breathing, followed by a low rumbling, almost demonic kind of sound—that is until I figured out I had recorded me falling asleep and then snoring.

I found a schematic diagram in a book which the author claimed had helped him get clear EVPs. I bought everything listed and asked a friend of mine to put it together for me.

When he brought it back to me two days later, it was small metal box with an antenna sticking out of it and a wire that I was supposed to plug into my recording device. I plugged it into my cassette recorder. When I played back the recordings, all I heard was even more static than the previous recordings I made. To say I was disappointed is an understatement. I decided to quit trying.

I then read an article about how people were returning a certain model of digital recorder because of voices people were hearing on them that shouldn't have been there. The recorders were pulled off the shelves for being "defective." EVP researchers thought they knew what was going on, and they bought up the recorders that hadn't yet been returned by stores to the manufacturers.

I decided I wanted one too, but I couldn't find one, so I bought a Sony digital recorder because it was recommended by the salesperson for its quality of recordings. When I got it home and took it out of its package, I set the time on the clock and forgot about it. I wasn't going to set myself up for another disappointing session.

I did bring it with me when I went out to California to visit my family. While I was out there, I also went to San Diego because I wanted to visit the Whaley House, which, according to the U.S. Department of Commerce, is the most haunted house in America.

The Whaley House is now a museum, so I had to buy a ticket to get in. In order to get one, I found out that I had to go to the official Whaley House store that sold not only tickets, but also Whaley house T-shirts, cups, postcards, etc. I bought a ticket and a T-shirt. I asked the young lady behind the register if she had had any ghostly experiences, and she admitted that if she had, she would have probably quit on the spot. I laughed with her, but it was hardly what I was hoping to hear.

I went next door to the museum, showed my ticket to the docent, and walked around the first floor. There was a photo album filled with pictures taken by visitors to the museum. Most of them were of orbs, which really didn't interest me. There were also letters written by people who apparently had had paranormal experiences such as smelling cigar smoke even though smoking in the house is prohibited.

I decided to go upstairs. The docent and I were the only two people in the house so it was quiet except for the street noises coming through the open door. As I walked up the stairs, I pulled out my digital recorder, hit the record button for thirty seconds, turned it off, and put it back in the pocket of my sports coat, promptly forgetting all about it.

I was back in Denver for more than a week when I remembered making the recording. The recorder was still in the pocket of my coat. I pulled it out and turned it on not expecting to hear anything. For twenty seconds there was only static. I was feeling relieved that I had made only a thirty-second recording when I heard a woman cry out, then scream, "Oh God! Please no! I can't!"

I couldn't believe it! I had my first EVP recording! I kept playing the recording over and over again, not sure I believed what I was hearing. I played it for other people to see if they heard what I had heard. They did. I can't tell you how excited I was!

After that, it seemed that every time I turned on a recorder during an investigation, I was capturing EVPs. When I asked people to listen to them, some of them suggested I was recording stray radio transmissions. I thought that might have been a possibility so I started asking questions, then paused for ten seconds, and asked another question. When I listened to the recordings, I was stunned that occasionally, not always, I actually heard answers to my questions!

For example, here's a sample of an EVP I captured at the Lumber Baron Inn, here in Denver.

Me—Is there anyone here?
Female voice—Yes!
Me—How did you die?
Female voice—I was murdered!

When I visited the inn, it was a bed and breakfast. Back in the 70s it was an apartment building, and two young women were found murdered in one of the apartments. When I was there, the murders still hadn't been solved.

One year, on President's Day, a friend named Diane called me and asked if I would go with her to a local cemetery that had a reputation for being haunted. She had the day off and had wanted to go to this cemetery for years, but no one would go with her. I didn't want to go with her either, but I had nothing going on that day, so I went. I grabbed a mini-cassette recorder, and Diane and I went "ghost hunting."

There's a section of the cemetery that is reserved for Civil War soldiers, and I got the idea to conduct a "roll call." I called out the names I saw on a dozen stones trying as best I could to sound like a military officer. Before I did, I looked around to make sure Diane wasn't around. I didn't want her to say something into her own recorder that might be picked up by mine.

After I finished calling out names, I left my recorder on for a couple of minutes longer. I then turned it off, put it in my jacket pocket, and went off to find Diane. We agreed to call it a day, and Diane drove me back home.

I was sitting at my desk writing an account of the day to post on the Web site I had at the time. I was pleased to hear three responses to my "roll call."

"Here!"

"Yes, sir!"

"Present!"

What I heard next caused chills to go up and down my spine. I couldn't believe what I was hearing so I rewound the recording. When I heard it a second time, I said, out loud, "No way!"

I rewound it again and played it back. "Oh hell no!" was my reaction this time.

I sat back in my chair. I couldn't believe what I was hearing, but I couldn't deny it either; the recording was so clear. First I heard the wind blowing; then, as if someone were standing next to me, I heard a woman calling out, "An ... tha ... nee!"

And it wasn't Diane's voice.

Chapter

7

I had a ghost-hunting group at this time, and people were constantly contacting me, wanting to join. For the most part, anyone who asked was welcomed to join. I received an email from a woman named Lauren who had heard about my group, what we were doing, and wanted to be a part of it.

After talking to each other on the phone, we agreed to meet for coffee and a face-to-face chat. Lauren was charming, easy to talk to, and eager to learn. I knew she'd be a great addition to my group and asked her to join us.

"Have you ever thought about appearing on a television show?"

she asked me after doing a few investigations with me. I admitted I had but hadn't pursued it.

"Would you mind if I tried for you?" she asked.

"Sure," I said. "On one condition, if you get me on a show, you have to do it with me." I thought the idea of appearing on television would discourage her from following through with her idea.

Wouldn't you know it? Two days later she told me she had booked us on a local television show, and we were supposed to be on in just a few days! I didn't think about it at the time, but the day we were going to be on the show was Halloween, so it was a good fit to have a couple of ghost hunters on the show. They wanted "evidence" that they could present on the show to support our claims, so I gave Lauren a couple of EVPs they could play.

When the show teased our appearance, Jennifer, a friend of mine, happened to be watching where she worked. She's a dental hygienist and told her patient, "My friend Anthony is a ghost hunter . . . oh my God, that's him!"

The interview went off better than I could have hoped for. The hosts, though skeptical, were open to what we had to say.

After Lauren and I left the station, I received a couple of phone calls. One was from my long-time friend, Camille, who had watched the show and was calling to tell us how well it went. The second one was from Jennifer. She and her husband, Mike, wanted to know if I'd come to their home for dinner. I said I'd be happy to.

Mike and I had first met at a Catholic church where he and I, along with Camille, volunteered as youth ministers. Mike and I became best friends until he met Jennifer and married her.

The night of the dinner we discussed ghosts and why they might exist. We also talked about the Catholic practice of praying for the souls in purgatory. According to the Catechism of the Catholic Church, purgatory is a process of "purification, so as to achieve the holiness necessary to enter the joy of Heaven," which is experienced by those "who die in God's grace and friendship, but still imperfectly purified." (CCC 1030) They told me that they prayed the rosary for those souls every night.

As we were talking about this, Mike reached into his pocket, pulled out his rosary, and handed it to me. I was holding it cupped in my hands when suddenly "information" starting coming to me. "Mike, did this originally belong to your mother?" I asked.

He nodded his head.

"Did your mother pass from cancer?" I asked. Again, he didn't say anything; he only nodded his head.

"Was she bedridden at home for around six months, then taken to a hospice?" Mike confirmed this with another nod of his head.

"I don't how to tell to you this," I continued, "but it's almost as though your mother herself is telling me all of this."

Jennifer jumped up from the table and left. When she came back, she handed me a gold-colored rosary and said, "It's my turn!"

As soon as I held the rosary, her father appeared in front of me almost like a hologram. "This belonged to your father," I offered.

"That's right!" Jennifer answered, smiling and nodding her head excitedly. I continue sharing the impressions I was receiving including one about a conversation Jennifer had had with one of her brothers over the phone just two nights before. "He's talking about the phone call you had with your brother about your inheritance."

Jennifer confirmed this and told me what she and her brother had talked about with regards to what his plan was to do with part of his inheritance. "If Dad knew, he'd roll in his grave," Jennifer said.

"He knows, and he's rolling." Jennifer and I both laughed. "I've got to tell you something. I don't know about you two, but this is freaking me out!"

Here I was, someone who made fun of psychics for years, acting as though I was a psychic! I had no idea what to make of it. Mike and Jennifer took it in stride.

A couple of days later I called Camille who had just returned from South Dakota where she had attended her own father's funeral. I told her what had happened at the dinner with Jennifer and Mike. We agreed to meet for coffee later that day.

While we were having coffee, I asked her how she was doing since the funeral and how she was doing in general. She answered by saying, "I want to talk about what happened with you at Mike and Jennifer's house during dinner!"

I was a little reluctant to talk about it since I wasn't really sure how to explain what had happened. Camille kept insisting I talk about it. "Well," I began, "I was holding Mike's rosary like this," picking Camille's keys up from the table, holding them in my cupped hands. Suddenly, I felt an energy coming from her keys and threw them back down on the table.

"What?" Camille asked.

"I felt some kind of energy coming from your keys when I was holding them," I told her.

"Well, pick them back up and tell me what you get!" she laughed.

I wasn't crazy about the idea, but I picked the keys up and held them. I suddenly became "aware" of her father's presence. "Your father's here," I said.

Camille clapped her hands together. "What is he saying?"

"He wants to answer the questions you and your sister have about what to do with his rentals." I told her.

"Maria and I were talking on the phone just last night, and we were wondering which properties Dad wanted us to sell and in what order!"

I looked up at Camille. Her eyes were wide with amazement. "Are you kidding me? You two talked about this just last night?" I asked.

"Yes! We kept saying that we wished Dad would have told us what he wanted before he died!" I don't know who was more stunned, Camille or I.

I passed on what I was "receiving," and Camille said that she and her sister had pretty much come to the same conclusion as I was telling her. I didn't know whether any of this really made sense to Camille or she just wanted it to make sense. I did describe an odd-shaped rental property her father owned. What I was seeing in my mind's eye was so strange that I used napkins to illustrate what I was talking about. I just couldn't believe a building would be built the way this one was.

"I know which unit you're talking about," Camille told me.

"Your dad really owned a rental that looks like this?" I asked.

"Exactly like that!" she said, laughing.

I shook my head. I couldn't believe what was happening even while it was happening.

Camille's husband, Steve, joined us a little while later, and Camille told him what had happened. Steve reacted with the skepticism I knew he would. "Give him a reading too!" Camille told me. Steve shook his head and said he didn't want one. To be honest, I didn't want to give him one, but Camille insisted, and I agreed, in part, because I wanted to get his reaction since he was so skeptical.

I gave him a "reading." Steve didn't really respond, so Camille confirmed or denied what I was saying. When I was done, Camille was excited about the reading, but Steve acted nonchalant and unimpressed. I asked Camille the next day if he had said anything, and she told me that he had thought I got most of the information I put out from her.

"You two talk to each other all of the time." Steve told Camille.

"Well, yeah, we do, but not about your family!"

"Well," Steve said, "no offense to Anthony, but I just don't believe anyone can talk to the dead."

"You're not upset about what Steve said, are you?" Camille asked.

"Not at all," I told her. "After all, I don't believe I was talking to your father either."

"Where do you think you were getting all of that from then?" Camille wondered, shocked about how skeptical I was about what I had done at the coffee shop.

I had given it a lot of thought, and the only answer I could come up with was "psychometry," gleaning information about a person by touching one of his or her personal objects. After all, I was holding rosaries that belonged to Mike's mother and Jennifer's father during the reading I gave them.

Then I was holding Camille's keys, and later, Steve's phone. It was the only "logical" answer I could come up with. I explained this to Camille and told her it's a supposed ability some psychics claimed to have. "Do you think you're a psychic?" she asked me.

I laughed. "No, I don't think I'm a psychic."

"Well, you're getting that information from somewhere," she said seriously, "and I don't think it's coming from you. I think it's coming from somewhere else."

I didn't know how to respond to that, so I let it go.

My Reading with Anthony
By Diane Padilla

I have known Anthony in a more or less professional capacity for several years. One day he was relating to me how he had unexpectedly been given the gift of mediumistic ability, and so I asked him to do a reading for me.

I was admittedly skeptical as many people are when dealing with mediums, especially after having known Anthony for a while. I simply could not imagine that this person, who was so skeptical about psychics, had such a talent. But I guess it isn't for me to judge! All I can do is to relate my experiences.

I was out of contact with Anthony for about a year and a half when we finally reconnected; he told me how this extraordinary event had transpired. Basically, the ability hit him out of the blue, without him seeking it or even understanding it. As I said, I was skeptical but asked him to do a reading for me, more out of curiosity than anything else. We arranged to meet for lunch the following week, and he agreed to do a reading at that time.

A little background is necessary in order to fully appreciate the entire scenario. I had been a state employee for about ten years and had quit just a couple of months before I called Anthony. At the time he did my reading, I was working in a warehouse and had been troubled by horrendous headaches from the day I'd started there. We were convinced that the cause was mold or something similar in our building as all three employees were troubled by symptoms of sick building syndrome.

Because the headaches had become debilitating, I sought medical care and went through a battery of tests, including an MRI, before the doctor concluded that she simply did not know what was causing them. Anthony had no knowledge of this whatsoever and I am 100 percent certain of that fact.

At the beginning of the reading, he mentioned a couple in Indian (Native American) clothing that he said identified themselves as my grandparents. The grandparents that I did know both had Indian blood but were not full bloods and certainly did not dress in Indian clothing, so I basically just told him to come back to them later.

He identified a Mexican man who was related to me, describing him as a person with a square jaw and pencil thin mustache who worked with his hands. Since I was half Mexican, this information could be anyone, and so I was still skeptical until he said the word "tio" which in Spanish means "uncle." He then went on to say that this man had lived in California and that his wife was still alive. This fit my Uncle Dave to a T. Many other details did as well. Still . . . it could be coincidence, lucky guesses, or something else.

The turning point in the reading came when he said that Uncle Dave, and all of my other relatives who had passed on, (and there are *a lot*) were worried about "something to do with your head." He then went on to say that, although it didn't make sense, this long dead, mostly Spanish speaking man was showing him an MRI machine! I had had my MRI just the week before, and no one, other than my kids and one friend, knew. Not even my husband knew I was having the test done! There is absolutely no way that this man, whom I hadn't even seen in years, could have known this; absolutely none at all.

Okay, so I was convinced, but the question still remained, who were the people in Indian clothing? He went back to this and again said they were my grandparents and functioned more or less as guides or guardian angels. Then it fell into place for me. In the Indian cultures, any elder is considered a grandparent, so it didn't necessarily mean they were blood kin. Not that I would know as I had never known my birth father who had the highest percentage of Indian blood in my background. I kept questioning Anthony, and he kept telling me that the man was wearing a feathered headdress, but it wasn't the stereotypical type seen on TV and in movies. It finally hit me whom he was talking about!

Years ago, I had been a dancer with an Aztec dance troupe. At one of our performances, in two different photographs, the face of an Aztec Eagle Warrior had shown up behind me. I figured that he was the Mexican version of a guardian angel and never really thought a whole lot about it. The warrior had actually been seen by a couple of people as well, so I knew that he was there. I emailed Anthony a photo of an Aztec dancer, and he verified that it was indeed the type of headdress he'd seen. A week or two later I was finally able to show him the pictures of the warrior behind me when I was dancing and he confirmed that was the person he had seen. All I can say now is . . . I'm a believer!

*   *   *

Chapter

8

I didn't give a lot of thought to what had happened at the dinner with Jennifer and Mike or with Camille and Steve. My focus continued to be investigating reports of hauntings and apparitions with my group . . . until the day that would change my life.

Cheryl and I had become friends a few years before when we began talking to each other at a barbeque. Even though she had an interest in what I was doing, she always had declined my invitations to join an investigation. She did, however, enjoy hearing about them. One day Cheryl said, "Anthony, I need to talk to you." She took me aside from the people I was talking to. "Sarah is dead."

I knew she wasn't kidding, but for a moment it just didn't seem real. Sarah was one of those people I thought would be around forever. As long as I had known her, all she ever wanted was to be a mother. On the day I was told of her death, she was the mother of a two-year-old daughter and a six-month-old son.

"What happened?" I asked. Cheryl told me that Sarah's parents were visiting from another state and suggested that Sarah and her husband go out to dinner. Sarah joined her husband at a restaurant after he had gotten off work. After they had finished eating, they were going home in separate cars when a freak accident involving another car killed Sarah instantly while her husband, who was driving behind her, watched helplessly.

By this time, as a result of my investigations and EVP experiments, I believed that those who have died can indeed hear us. I still didn't believe they could talk to us, other than through EVPs. While I was on my way to her memorial service, I started talking out loud to Sarah. "Sarah, I just want to tell you how sorry I am about what has happened to you. I'm still having a hard time accepting it. I love you; I loved our friendship, and I'm going to miss you terribly."

Suddenly, I was aware, more than that, I knew that she was right next to me. "Hi, Anthony," I heard, not with my ears, but in my mind. "I loved our friendship, too. Thank you for being who you are. I'll miss you, too. By the way, tell my family I'm okay!" With that she was gone.

I didn't know what to think about what had just happened. Was it really Sarah or simply my imagination? My first thought was that it was simply my imagination, but it was that last thing I heard that puzzled me. "Tell my family I'm okay!" I didn't really know Sarah's husband, and I didn't know her parents. Why would I imagine her saying that?

When I arrived at the church where her service was being held, the pictures of Sarah located in the lobby drove home the fact that she was indeed gone. That didn't mean it was really she who had talked to me, though, and not my imagination. I saw several friends there, and I went up to someone I felt I could trust. I wish I could remember who it was, but I was in such a daze, I don't. I do remember our conversation though.

"I was on my way here, and I think I heard from Sarah," I said "What did she say?" I was asked.

"She wants me to tell her family she's okay." I said sheepishly.

"Did you?" she asked.

"Did I what?" I asked, not sure what she meant.

"Tell her family she's okay," she said. I realized she wasn't joking.

"Are you kidding me? I'm not going to do that! For one thing, they're not going to believe me. Secondly, they'll think I'm nuts!"

She shrugged her shoulders, and said, "I think you should tell them. After all, it's what Sarah asked you to do," before she walked away.

I went up to two more friends, told them what had happened and had almost the exact same conversation. I was honestly hoping that someone would tell me that it was just my imagination and not to worry about it. I was hoping they would agree with me that telling Sarah's family was a bad idea. I decided to try one more time.

I walked up to Cheryl—the same Cheryl who had told me about Sarah's passing. "I was on my way over here and Sarah came to me. She talked to me."

"What did she say?" Cheryl asked.

"She wants me to tell her family that she's okay."

"Did you?" Cheryl asked.

"Why is everyone asking me this?" I wondered. I began to feel frustrated that no one was telling me I simply imagined the conversation.

"No, I didn't tell them. They'll think I'm crazy!" I told Cheryl exasperated.

"Why?" she asked, "that's your thing isn't it, talking to dead people?" With that she walked away.

I called out after her, "What do you mean talking to dead people is my thing?"

She simply kept walking. Without turning around she waved and said, "Go tell them, Anthony!"

I didn't tell her family Sarah wanted them to know she was okay. Whether or not they would have thought I was crazy wasn't the point. I wasn't sure I hadn't lost my mind.

Chapter

9

No matter how hard I tried, I couldn't get out of my mind what had happened the day of Sarah's memorial service or what Cheryl had said to me. Was I really talking to Sarah? More to the point, was it possible that Sarah was really talking to me?

I knew from reading books about paranormal investigations that there were people who claimed to speak to the dead and that they were referred to as "mediums." I bought a book about psychic medium George Anderson, entitled *We Don't Die*. I read hoping to understand what mediumship was about and if it's indeed possible. George's ability showed itself when he was a young boy after he had recovered from a serious illness.

That was hardly the case with me, so I decided to take another route to try to understand what was going on. I decided to do "readings" for complete strangers over the Internet. I thought if I did one hundred of these readings, I'd know, one way or the other, if I really was able to speak to people who had passed away.

I set up an account on Yahoo Messenger, and I posted messages on a number of different sites offering to do readings for free. I stated that if people wanted a reading, they were to let me know by sending an email, sharing only their first name. The people were not to indicate to me any information such as name, gender, or relationship about whom they wanted to reconnect with. Stating any one of these facts would disqualify them from receiving a reading.

I had no clue if it was even possible to do readings like this over the Internet, but I did it to satisfy my own skepticism. I also didn't want to receive any clues such as people nodding or shaking their heads in response to what I was saying. Besides, I thought, if this ability were real, souls would be able to find me in Denver, Colorado, no matter where the loved ones they were trying to reconnect with were living.

When the time came for my first appointment, I was nervous because I had no clue as to what was going to happen. I hadn't received a reading from a medium before, and all that I knew about what a reading might be like came from what I had read in Anderson's book. I told myself that if the session was a complete fiasco, it would be all right since I wasn't a medium anyway and made that clear in my postings.

My first reading was for a woman who had three children, all of whom had passed away—one by suicide, one in an accident, and the other from cancer. As soon as we started messaging, I saw a "picture" in my mind's eye of a young man in a football uniform. I was stunned when she told me that one of her son's played football. "Please tell my mom that I'm sorry."

"He wants you to know how sorry he is about what he did," I wrote. What did he do? I wondered. I immediately felt myself become angry and depressed. That's when I understood that he had taken his own life. "Did your son take his own life?" I wrote.

"Yes, he did," she wrote back after several moments of silence. After that, I relayed everything thought, feeling, and impression that came to me. I was stunned at how much of what I told her made sense to her.

Towards the end of the session she asked me if she could ask her children one question: "Why couldn't she feel their presence anymore?"

I typed the first thing that came to me. She needed to learn to stand on her own two feet. They hadn't left her and would always be with her, but she had to learn how to walk through her grief. They told her that they wanted her to move on with her life.

It was at that moment she became angry with me and began to doubt everything I had said up to this point in the session—all of which she had previously confirmed. I decided to end the session as quickly as I could.

After I logged off, I spent some time thinking about the reading. All in all, I thought it had gone well, but I just wasn't sure what it all had meant.

Were three young boys who had passed away really communicating with their mother through me? Was what happened during the session real? Or was it the result of a mother who so desperately wanted to hear from her sons that she confirmed what I told her they were saying because she needed to believe they really were communicating with her through me?

I still didn't know what to think or believe. I hoped that the appointments other people had booked with me for an online reading would help me figure things out, one way or the other.

Several years later I visited Lily Dale, a spiritualist community in New York. I wanted to see the famous "stump," which is literally a tree stump on which various mediums over the years have stood on to give readings. Doing this is considered an honor and can be done only by invitation of the community.

In front of the stump talking was gathered a large group of people, composed of almost entirely women, with the exception of a single male, so I sat on one of the benches and waited. Eventually the crowd started slowly breaking up, and a woman began walking towards me.

"Pardon me," I said to her, "but may I ask what's going on?"

"It's a class," she responded, her voice barely above a whisper.

"What kind of class?" I whispered back, leaning forward to make sure she could hear me, not really sure why we were whispering.

"It's a class on mediumship. We're learning how to be mediums," she whispered again, but I could hear the pride in her voice and see it on her face.

"Wow!" I said, continuing to whisper. "How long is the class?"

"Two years, and it's not easy to get into." I nodded, thanked her for her time, and she walked away.

I continued to sit there thinking about how I had started doing readings over the Internet without any formal instruction and that my training was done on the job and had been provided by the souls who were communicating through me. After everyone was gone, I walked up to the stump and found it was encased in concrete to protect it. It was also surrounded by a small fence. I thought about stepping over the fence and standing on the stump but decided against it out of respect. I did wonder if I'd ever be invited to deliver messages on it someday. [Anthony was indeed invited to read on the stump in August of 2012.]

Chapter

10

Looking back at the time, I realize now how patient the souls were in helping me overcome my own skepticism. Things would happen during a reading that I simply could not explain, other than to say that the information was really coming from the Other Side.

Most of the readings I did online were for women, so I was surprised to see a man requesting a session with me. I don't remember his name, but I'll call him Paul. During Paul's reading, his father came through. I told Paul that his father was telling me he had loved the outdoors and had loved to hunt. I also told him that his father was showing me a bear paw. I had no idea what that meant, and Paul wasn't saying. After his father pulled his energy away, Paul told me that just before his father died, he gave Paul his most prized possession— the paw of a bear he killed.

Another thing I noticed was that the souls were apparently using my own life experiences in order to convey messages to their loved ones. Books I had read, movies I had watched, conversations I had had with friends, would all become fair game for them to use during sessions.

I received an email from a woman named Natalie, who told me I had done a reading for a friend of hers and that her friend spoke highly of me and the session. She asked me if I would do a reading for her, but she wanted me to do her reading over the phone instead of over Yahoo Messenger. I was a bit nervous, since I hadn't done a phone reading before. I decided to go ahead and do it because during the Internet readings messages were starting to come faster than I could type.

"I have a young lady here who passed from leukemia," I told her.

"That's my daughter," she said and began to cry.

"Your daughter is showing me two characters from one of my favorite television sitcoms *The King of Queens*. One of them is Carrie."

"That's my daughter's name," she said.

"She's telling me that your father is with her. Now she's showing me Arthur, another character from the same show."

"That's my father's name."

Without thinking, I blurted out, "Are you bullshitting me?"

"No," she laughed. "I'm not."

I couldn't help but wonder if I were just getting information by somehow reading people's minds during their session. Not that I actually believed mind reading was possible, but it made more sense to me than the idea that I was actually hearing from dead people. Then I did a reading for a woman named Kim.

This was the first session I did during which information came through that was not intended for the person I was doing the reading for but for someone else. In this case, it was Kim's next door neighbor whose husband had died in a motorcycle accident.

"Did his wife take him off of life support?" I asked her.

"Yes."

"The reason why I'm asking is that he's showing me a celery stalk. I have no idea what that means except that he's glad he didn't continue living his life as a vegetable."

Kim told me later that she had talked to her neighbor about the reading and what I had said about seeing a celery stalk. Her neighbor said that it made perfect sense. A year before her husband died, a friend of his, who also rode on a motorcycle, was in an accident, and his wife couldn't bring herself to take him off life support. They were talking about this when her husband said, "If that ever happens to me, I want you to pull the plug. I don't want to live as a vegetable. That last thing I want is to be a celery stalk."

Kim told me that she had no idea they had had that conversation. I scratched mind reading off the list as a possible explanation and for the first time started to think that souls on the Other Side might be communicating through me after all.

My Reading with Anthony

By Sheryl Wagoner-Dunn

I met Anthony Quinata through a local psychic medium, the late Natalie Smith-Blakeslee, at a taping of her television show. I'd received many readings before, but when Anthony looked at me that night and started talking about a young man who had taken his own life with a gun and had a bad boy attitude, I immediately knew whom he was talking about.

Anthony said that this man had had problems with drinking and drugs and that he wanted me to pass messages on to someone who was still here. He described this person as a "mother figure" to him. He wanted her to know that he had appreciated her efforts in trying to help him while he was alive but that he "just couldn't take the bullshit anymore."

This guy lived in my neighborhood, growing up where he and his family were friends of my brothers and sisters. He was always at the beach in cutoff shorts and drinking beer while he wore a leather jacket like "the Fonz" in colder weather. Even though he was older and I didn't know him well, he was always friendly to me.

He died about fifteen years ago, but never in my wildest dreams did I ever think he would come through during a reading I was receiving. Anthony told me that it was because he wanted me to be a medium and pass the message along. I didn't know how I was supposed to do that since I hadn't seen anyone in his family for years.

The next day I was shopping for groceries when I ran into his oldest sister . . . the woman he referred to as the "mother figure!" His mother had passed away before he did, and his sister took on the responsibility of raising him. It was years since I had last seen her, and I wasn't sure she would even remember me, let alone believe what I about to tell her.

Thankfully, although she was shocked, she did listen to what I passed along to her from her brother and even welcomed it. She told me that she had tried so hard to help him with his problems and had even tried getting professional help, but it wasn't enough. Even though she kept thanking me and told me what I passed along had helped her, I walked away hoping that she didn't think I was some crazy woman.

I've received other readings from Anthony since, and my brother, who had thought before he passed away that psychics and mediums were all in league with the devil, came through with details about his life, apologizing for his last days. I was shocked not only by the accuracy of what Anthony told me, but by the fact that he would often come through during the readings Anthony gave to other people who knew him. He's always trying to make amends during these readings. "How can this be the work of the devil?" I've often asked myself.

Thank you, Anthony, for your beautiful abilities and the work you do. You've brought comfort not only to me but also to my family and friends who have received a reading from you as well.

*   *   *

Chapter

11

I had originally set a goal of doing one hundred readings online before deciding whether or not I was actually communicating with souls on the Other Side. Since I wasn't keeping track, I don't know how many I had actually done, but the last one was with a young woman named Marie.

"Marie, your grandmother wants me to tell you that Heaven is real. Heaven does exist!"

"When my grandmother was dying," Marie told me, "everyone in my family got a chance to spend about twenty minutes alone with her. When it was my turn, I couldn't stop crying. I was so scared. I believed in

God, but I didn't know if I would ever see my grandmother again. Even though she was in a coma, I told her that my belief in God was being shaken. I said to her that if there was any way she could communicate with me after she died to tell me that Heaven is real and that it exists, I needed her to do that. I needed to know that I'd see her again!"

"Well, it looks like your prayer was answered," I told her.

We chatted for a while longer about her grandmother and the reading. When we said good-bye, I thought that was the end of that. I didn't expect to hear from her again. I was wrong.

Two days later, I was sitting in a coffee shop when I received from Marie an instant message on my computer. "Anthony, I need you to call me. Here's my phone number. Call me as soon as possible!" Earlier that day I'd had a feeling I was going to hear from Marie again, so I was ready when it came. I called her.

"Anthony, I need to ask you something, and I need you to tell me the truth. *Do not* lie to me," she said. "Were you talking to my grandmother?"

"The truth is," I told her, "I don't know."

"What do you mean you don't know?" she screamed into the phone.

"Look," I said, "I didn't know your grandmother, and I don't know you. I just passed on what I receiving." She started to sob. "Marie, you wanted me to tell you the truth, and that's the truth. If I was standing in front of a firing squad, and I was told, 'We're going to ask you a question. If you don't answer, you die. If you lie, you die. Were you talking to Marie's grandmother?' I would tell them what I told you, 'I don't know.'

"If the same firing squad were to say to me, 'One more question and, again, if you lie, you die . . . do you *think* you were talking to Marie's grandmother?' I would say, 'Yes, I do.' Marie, it was more like I was listening to your grandmother and passing along to you what I was hearing. That's all I did." As soon as I said that, I thought to myself, "Did I just admit to being a medium?"

Marie then shared with me that she had told her father about her session with me and how she had heard from his mother. She thought that he'd be excited, but instead he became outraged and told her what I did was "evil."

That's why Marie was questioning whether or not I was communicating with her grandmother. Her father told her that I was conversing with the devil himself. "Marie," I told her, "if the messages are coming from Satan, or his demons, as your father is claiming, then they're not doing a very good job. All of the messages I've been passing on are of love, hope, and healing."

Thankfully, that seemed to calm her down. After we said our good-byes, I realized that being a medium carried a huge responsibility and it was one I wasn't sure that I wanted.

Chapter

12

After the phone call with Marie, I was ready to be done with the whole "medium thing." After all, I wasn't trying to prove anything, only understand what had happened the night of Sarah's memorial service. It's not that I felt I understood anything a whole lot more than I did that night, but in my mind I was finished. I just wanted to go back to investigating hauntings and such with my group.

Matt, a member of my group, told me that he knew three people who were interested in joining us to do investigations and asked if I would mind meeting them. I suggested that we do so over lunch.

When we got together the next day, we made small talk as we looked over the menu. After we ordered, I blurted out, "Someone's grandmother wants to make a connection." Everyone looked at me, but no one said anything. Matt started looking nervous and uncomfortable. I don't think he had told his friends anything about me and the whole "talking to dead people" thing.

I knew that if I were going to be able to eat lunch in peace, I had to pass on what this particular soul was telling me. "Did one of you collect baseball cards as a child?"

They looked at one another, but no one said anything. "I'm told that one of you had a nickname that involved being smacked." No one claimed that one either. Everyone looked at me, looked at each other, and started playing with their napkins.

"Now I'm being told to say the name, 'Sylvia.'"

This time Matt spoke up. "I think you're talking to me," he said. "I have an aunt named Sylvia."

"Your grandmother wants to know why you haven't finished school and when you plan to finish. She says that education is very important, and you need to finish school."

Matt laughed and looking embarrassed, said, "That would be my grandmother. Education was very important to her, and I didn't finish getting my degree."

He then told us that the rest of what I said made sense too. When he was ten years old, he had collected baseball cards for a period of time, but he didn't think about it when I said it. He also said that his mother used to talk with her hands all of the time. Whenever she spoke and her hands started flying, he couldn't help but flinch occasionally. His grandmother thought it was so funny that she nicknamed him "Rodger Dodger."

While Matt was telling us all of that, I couldn't help but think of what Michael Corleone had said in the movie *Godfather III*. "Just when I thought I was out, they pull me back in!"

By the way, in case you're wondering, none of Matt's friends joined our group after that.

My Reading with Anthony
By Matt Uney

I just wanted to take a few moments to tell you about my reading from Anthony Quinata. I was fortunate enough to spend a few minutes with Anthony, and he was kind enough to do a reading for me. We were having lunch at a restaurant with three other people, and what he started to pick up on was a relative of mine.

He had mentioned that someone was talking to him about baseball, and he wanted to know who that was. None of us answered at first.

Then he mentioned that there was something about a nickname and it had to do with being smacked. Still, nobody mentioned anything.

Then he mentioned that the female to whom he was speaking had a relative named Sylvia. That was the moment when things came together, and I told him he might be picking up on one of my dead relatives.

When I was a boy, I used to spend the summers down in Eads, Colorado, with my Grandmother Clara. During that time, which was around 1988, I briefly started to collect baseball cards and spent a lot of time at my grandparent's house sorting them and putting them in binders.

The nickname thing also made sense. When I would get into trouble, my mother would sometimes spank me when I needed it. One thing that would amuse my grandmother was when my mother would be talking and using hand gestures, I would flinch sometimes. My grandmother then gave me the nickname "Roger Dodger."

My grandmother had a few siblings, and one of her sisters was named Sylvia. This is when I knew that Anthony was speaking to my grandmother. He mentioned a few things that were nice to hear, such as how my grandmother loved me. He also mentioned that she was a little frustrated that I hadn't finished college. This made me laugh because that was just like her. She always used to be on me to do better in school and to go as far as I could.

Anthony also mentioned my mother and something she does in an almost ritualistic way. It is an activity that makes my grand-mother happy. As a result, she wants my mother to know how it makes her feel and that she loves my mother.

A week later I spoke with my mother and asked her if any of what Anthony shared made sense. She told me that she prays to my grandmother every day, and it is something she has done since her death in 1987.

I have known Anthony for a little over a year. I haven't col-lected baseball cards for over ten years. Nobody knows about my childhood with my grandparents, and nobody knew about my mother and her prayers. It was very enlightening to experience a reading from Anthony. It is an experience I will never forget.

*   *   *

Chapter

13

Word started getting out among my friends about what I was doing. Many of them received readings regardless of whether or not they had asked for one.

I was having lunch one day with Tamela, who was not only a friend but also a member of my ghost hunting group, when she received a reading from me. I'll let her tell you what happened in her own words:

My Reading with Anthony
By Tamela Burkhe

During my reading with Anthony, I was very tight-lipped. I knew that people draw out information from you, so I gave him only yes or no answers or shrugs. Anthony knew a lot about my parents and brother, but nothing about my extended family. My parents and brother are still alive, but I have lost many relatives whom I have never spoken about. My mother has a big family, and my father's family has experienced many losses in the past few years.

The information he gave me was staggering. He told me that my grandmother on my mother's side was there to speak to me. She told Anthony that she did not know me when she was alive and that she was sad about that fact. He was completely accurate. My grandmother had severe dementia. She was catatonic by the time I was born. I would see her sitting on the couch at my grandfather's house, but she did not "know" me and I didn't know her. Then my father's mother came through. In contrast, Anthony told me that this grandmother had been very active in my life and was still helping me from the Other Side. He told me that I had been her favorite grandchild. He was right. I had been that grandmother's favorite. I had also seen her in many of my dreams since her death. Many times she was there to comfort me through a difficult patch in my life.

He also told me that she had gone with me in spirit on a cruise after my breakup with a guy she referred to as "the dork." I laughed. This had happened long after she had passed. A guy had broken up with me for strange reasons. At the time I referred to him as "the dork" for about a year after that. A few months after the breakup, I went on a European cruise. The only cruise I had ever been on then or since. I had felt very lonely without him there. I didn't meet Anthony for another six years after that cruise. I never mentioned it or "the dork." It was great to hear from Anthony that my grandmother had been watching over me during that time.

Anthony then moved on to my grandfather on my dad's side. He said that he had a message for me that only I would understand. Anthony said that my grandfather was showing him a rifle and a deer. I laughed. My grandfather used to play a joke on me. He would look out the window and tell me that he was going "dear hunting." Then he would shout, "There's a dear!" and seem to point out the window. I'd crane my head to look out the window, trying to find the deer. When I couldn't find it, I'd look back at my grandfather, and he'd be pointing to himself.

Then my aunt came through. Anthony described her as quite a character. He said she was pushy, loud, boisterous, and lovable. She was. He said that she had died of lung cancer. She did. He said she was pissed about it because it should not have happened. She said the doctors had messed up. It was true. They had seen a small spot on her lung the year before. It was on the outside of the lung. The doctors dismissed it as a shadow. A year later when they x-rayed again, it was throughout her lungs. It was too late then. It had been stage I the year before. When they had finally decided to treat her, it was already stage III. It had been a tragedy.

He read a number of relatives for me that day. At the end, he was about to finish the reading when he said, "Wait a minute."

He told me that there was one more person there. He'd been there waiting through the entire reading. Anthony said he had been so quiet that he almost didn't realize the man was there. This was my uncle, and he had passed recently. He said because my uncle was such a quiet man, people would almost forget that he was in the room. He never talked much. Even in this reading he just stepped forward, showed Anthony some pink roses for me, and then stepped back to disappear. Anthony said that he had died of intestinal problems.

My uncle Neil had died just a few months before. He was such a quiet man that I don't think I heard him say more than twenty words in all the time I knew him. He died of colon cancer.

* * *

A few days later I received a "thank you" card in the mail from Tamela. I opened the card, and inside was a check for a sizable amount of money. She wrote a note thanking me for her reading and said that one third of the check was for the reading. The other two thirds was payment if I agreed to do readings for her friends at her birthday party which was coming up in a couple of weeks.

I hadn't received a dime for all of the readings I had done up until that point and had no plans to charge for a reading either. Of course, I didn't plan on doing readings up to this point either. I considered, for about two seconds, giving Tamela her check back before deciding against it and agreeing to do the readings at her party.

The night of the party I introduced myself by saying, "My name is Anthony, and I'm a psychic medium. I'm like a bridge between those who have passed on to the Other Side and the loved ones they left behind. Now, most people hire a clown to entertain at their birthday party, but Tamela hired me to . . . hey!" Everyone got a good laugh at that one. I told them a little of my story and began the readings.

The first person I read that night was a woman whom I won't name. I told her that her grandmother was coming through and had a message for "Antonio." "I don't know an Antonio," she replied.

"Think about it for a moment, because your grandmother is insisting that you do. Now she's telling me that Antonio is your father."

"My father's name isn't Antonio. I don't know who you're talking about."

"Is your father down in Pueblo (Colorado), right now, as we speak? That's what your grandmother is telling me."

"No," she replied. "He's at home." I could tell that people at the party were beginning to enjoy the idea that the guy who could supposedly speak to dead people was getting everything wrong.

I decided to move on and read three more people. Thankfully, the readings went much better with them. I still felt frustrated about the first reading though.

Tamela called me a few days later and told me that the woman I read told her mother about the reading the next day. She told her mother that I said her grandmother wanted to pass a message on to "Antonio" and how she didn't know anyone named Antonio.

"That's your father. His name is Antonio," her mother told her.

"Then why does everyone call him "Tony?" she asked. (I swear to you that this is what Tamela told me this person asked her mother.)

"That's his nickname. Everyone called him Tony, except your grandmother. She always called him Antonio." It also turned out that her father *was* in Pueblo on business the night of Tamela's birthday party.

Tamela thought it was a lot funnier than I did. She also told me that a couple of people asked her how much I charged for readings, and she wanted to know if it was okay for her to give them my number. I still hadn't given any thought about charging for doing readings. Tamela encouraged me to do so, saying that her friends could afford to pay for a reading and that I should be charging for them. I decided to charge one-hundred dollars a session.

I was still receiving requests for readings online. When I started telling people that I wasn't doing them for free, but for a fee, those requests slowly but surely stopped coming. On the other hand, the more readings I did for a fee, the more referrals I received. What originally started out as an experiment was becoming a full-blown occupation.

Chapter

14

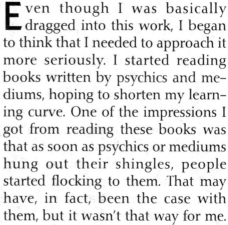

Even though I was basically dragged into this work, I began to think that I needed to approach it more seriously. I started reading books written by psychics and mediums, hoping to shorten my learning curve. One of the impressions I got from reading these books was that as soon as psychics or mediums hung out their shingles, people started flocking to them. That may have, in fact, been the case with them, but it wasn't that way for me.

I had business cards printed and a promotional photo taken of me. A friend of mine, Rachel, helped me create my first Web site.

I did a reading for a woman who

owned a local weekly newspaper. She was so impressed that she asked me if she could run an ad for me in her paper for six months at no charge. Since I wouldn't have to pay for it, I told her to go for it.

I bought books about how to market myself. I bought one promising to teach me how to book myself solid with appointments. I did virtually everything that it suggested. I then sat back and waited for the appointments to roll in. And I waited some more. Instead of getting more clients due to my brilliant marketing efforts, the phone calls stop coming—even the referrals stopped coming.

My expenses, however, kept coming. The money I had saved, and was now living on, was disappearing fast. At first, I panicked. Then I became angry. I began to wonder if this was some sort of cosmic joke that God and the souls were playing on me. I didn't want to do this work to begin with, and when I had finally decide to commit myself to doing it full time, people stopped wanting readings from me!

It didn't take long for me to decide that I'd had enough. I told God that I was done. I quit. I wasn't doing "the work" anymore. I told the souls I was through. I wanted them to leave me alone and to let me live my life in peace.

I stopped all of my marketing efforts. If anyone asked how things were going, I told them I wasn't doing that sort of work anymore.

That's when my phone started ringing again. People were calling wanting to book appointments for readings—sometimes within minutes of each other. What was going on?

The souls were letting me know that this wasn't about me. They let me know that no matter what I do or how hard I work, it'll never be enough. That's why no one responded to my marketing. People were hearing about me through a form of "spiritual marketing." No one came to me for a reading unless the souls of their loved ones had caused it to happen, and the waiting list of souls, who wanted to reconnect with their loved ones here, was long enough that they didn't need my "help."

The souls were also letting me know that while the person who made the appointment was paying me for my time, I was working for them. My only job consisted of listening, passing on the messages I was given, and learning. That was all. They'd take care of the rest.

Nothing, in my experience, demonstrated that decree as much as what happened over a five-month period of time. It began when a woman came to me for a reading. "Do you know someone named Jolyn?" I asked, spelling out the name. The woman said that she did. "Please tell her that I have someone here who wants to speak to her."

Two weeks later, just a couple of days before Halloween of 2007, a young woman named Jolyn came to see me along with her mother. Her mother's breast cancer had been in remission but had recently come back. She and her daughter were hoping to receive some advice from their loved ones who had passed on. (I want to interject a little sidenote here—*bad idea*. If you have a medical condition, seek advice from a medical professional, not someone who's passed on—even if that person had been a medical doctor while he/she was here.)

During their session I asked if either of them knew a woman named Laura. Jolyn said that she had a good friend named Laura, and I asked Jolyn to let Laura know that I had someone who wanted to speak to her.

About three weeks later I was doing a reading for a young woman named Laura. At the time I had already forgotten about the session with Jolyn and didn't put the two together. "I have a man here who is telling me he's your uncle. He's also showing me the NASA emblem. I want to say he's a rocket scientist. Does this make sense to you?" I asked her.

Laura nodded her head but didn't say anything.

"He's telling me jokes. *Horrible* jokes, but I've got to tell you that they're really humorous to him!"

Laura started laughing. "That's definitely my uncle! He used to tell me jokes that I didn't get, but he would laugh hysterically at!"

Laura's uncle mentioned that his wife had tried to commit suicide several times after his death. He asked that Laura ask her aunt to make an appointment with me so he could talk to her. She said she would pass the message along.

About a month later I was doing a reading for a woman named Sue, who told me that she was referred to me. When I asked referred her, she answered, "A friend," so I dropped it.

During the session her brother came through. He talked about how his wife had tried to commit suicide several times since he had died. He kept stressing he needed to talk to her.

After her brother pulled his energy back, I found out that Sue was Laura's mother. She then had to remind me who her daughter was and that her brother was the "rocket scientist" who told the bad jokes.

Three months later a young woman named Dawn came to see me with her son, her mother, and her fiancé. During this session Dawn's father came through. He talked about working for NASA as a scientist.

Now is a good time to tell you that when I do reading, I typically don't remember details later. Couple that with my insistence that no one who comes to see me tell me who they're there to reconnect with . . . to me a session is a session. Even though this was the third time I had someone come through with references to being a scientist who worked for NASA, I didn't put together that it was the same soul.

"Your father is telling me someone tried to shoot him/herself in the head. Do you know who this is?" I asked Dawn.

"Yes," she said, "it's my mother."

"I'm sorry, but who?" I asked, stunned.

"Me," her mother, who was quiet for most of the session, said. "I'm the one who tried to kill myself."

I turned my attention to her. "He's telling me that you've attempted suicide not just that one time, but several times. Is that true?" I asked.

"Yes, it's true," she said quietly. I noticed that for the first time in the session she had started to cry.

"He wants you to know that it's not the way to be with him

again. He wants you to stay here until it's your time. His job now is to help you through your journey . . . through your grief," I told her.

"I want to be with him," she said, tears streaming down her cheeks as the pain she was feeling inside started to come out.

"I understand you're hurting. Grief is another way of saying, 'I love you.'" I told her. "The end of grief in this world is life and happiness with your husband in the next. Please hold on until that day. Your husband wants you to know that when you're finished with your journey here, you'll see him again in a world of joy. I promise you will see him again. When you do, it'll be as though a second hasn't passed since the last time you saw him."

After our time together was over, I was concerned about them because they had a two-and-a-half-hour drive back home, and it was past six p.m. "You are stopping for dinner along your way home, right?" I asked (for people from Guam, it's all about food).

"Yes," Dawn said. "We're going to my Aunt Sue's house. She wants to hear how this went."

I shrugged my shoulders. "I don't know who she is," I told them.

"Yes, you do," Dawn insisted. "Sue Rodefer. You know . . . she's Laura's mom."

Suddenly, the entire chain of readings, starting with the one just before Halloween came back to me. "Oh my God!" was all I could say.

I hugged everyone good-bye and started to close up my office, marveling over everything that happened over the past five months. "You're good!" I said out loud, to both God, and Dawn's father. "You . . . are . . . good."

I received an email later that year from Dawn. It was one of those letters people send out around New Years, talking about the previous year. Dawn wrote that her mother was doing better. She seemed happier than she had in years. On a couple of occasions, they even caught her singing Christmas carols.

My Reading with Anthony
By Laura Rodefer

Let me start by saying that before I met with Anthony, I was not only an atheist but also more skeptical and cynical than anyone I knew. The only reason that I saw Anthony was that one of my best friends had seen him and he had asked if she knew someone by the name of Laura. He said that someone wanted to talk to me. My friend was also skeptic before she had met Anthony, so when she told me to see him, I thought I would go for laughs. I had seen a medium for fun before, and she was a joke. I had no expectations whatsoever and never dreamed that my life would be so changed after my visit.

Anthony started by saying that someone was coming through and identified himself as a space engineer. Anthony said he was "goofy." He said the man kept telling jokes that he would laugh at but weren't as funny to everyone around him as they were to him. That floored me because my Uncle Charles would call me on the phone, and when I answered, he would say "Hi Laura, this is Uncle Goofy." That was his style of humor. He would always tell jokes that he would laugh at, but others wouldn't laugh as hard as he would. My uncle also worked as an engineer for NASA.

Then Anthony said, "I have another man coming through wearing a coat that he's saying he's really proud of, but everyone else thinks is hideous, and he can't understand why."

Anthony was gesturing as though he were wearing a coat he was admiring exactly the way my father would have done when he had worn it.

I knew immediately that it was my father and that he was referring to a purple sports coat (I still have) that he was "awarded" by the company he worked for in recognition for having the highest sales figures the previous year.

Anthony asked about my aunt who had made several attempts at suicide. My uncle Goofy's wife had made several recent suicide attempts, including one with a gun in which she had shot herself from under her chin. Anthony asked about someone recently attempting suicide and made the hand gesture of a gun and put it under his chin as that is what he was seeing. My uncle wanted to get a message to my aunt not to commit suicide as she hadn't learned her lessons yet.

During my next visit Anthony said a man kept saying "wizard." I told him that I had no idea what wizard meant and to please move on. Anthony tried to move on, but the word "wizard" kept coming up in the reading. I later spoke with my mother and said that Anthony kept hearing the word wizard. She immediately knew it was my uncle because he had won the only Wizard Award ever given by NASA.

In this same visit, Anthony had said that someone kept saying the word *tor-till-la* which meant nothing to me. Confused, I told him to move on as I didn't have any association to the word tor-till-la. Later I spoke with my mother about the word tor-till-la and how it kept coming through in my session. My mother instantly told me that my father always pronounced the word tor-tilla incorrectly and that it was a big joke between them. A couple of days before I saw Anthony, my brother and my mom were talking about my dad. My mom was laughing and said that my dad never pronounced tortilla correctly. He would always sound out the LL's.

My father said that before he died, my mom asked, "What will I do without you?" He replied, "You will be fine." That is exactly what was said one day as my Mom and Dad were sitting at the kitchen table. I never knew about this conversation, and the wording was verbatim.

My father said that I was a tomboy and that he had always wanted me to be a girlie girl, but he lost the battle which was so true. Once again, he would use those exact words . . .

When my mother went to Anthony, someone came through and was calling herself "Eddie." It took my mom a while to remember that her mom used to call her cousin Elsie "Eddie." She said that my mom loved to play jacks and eat pancakes. Many years ago, Elsie had been visiting her, when my mom was playing jacks and they had pancakes for breakfast.

The name "Diamond Lil" came up in my mom's session as well. My mom said it was from her dad because when she was a teenager she would play poker with my dad and her dad nicknamed my mom "Diamond Lil."

Anthony has changed my life. I now know that there is life after what we know as death. I now KNOW that God exists and thank God daily for guiding me to Anthony.

*   *   *

Chapter

15

The next lesson I had to learn was that I'm only the instrument which the souls are using to communicate with their loved ones left behind. I don't need to understand the information that's being passed along, and they don't need my input or suggestions as to how to make the reading more meaningful for their loved ones. In other words, I'm not to get involved. I'm only supposed to listen and pass along what I get. Even so, there are times that I'm amazed by what evidence will be meaningful to someone.

Matt, the son of a friend of mine, flew into Denver from New York City to see his father. He was also hoping to be able to spend some time with me. I was invited to a party my friends were throwing, and I suggested that I show up early and do his reading before the other guests began arriving. They agreed it was a good idea.

When I got to their home, Matt and I went into a bedroom, and I began the session. He was hoping to hear from his grandmother, and she came through like gangbusters. She talked about their relationship before she died, and some of the things that have been going on in his life since she had passed. I told him at one point that she was giving me an "Italian vibe, but I don't think that she was Italian." I told him that she was saying she made Italian dishes more than she cooked Irish food. He laughed and agreed. He told me that even though she was Irish, she loved Italian food so much that she might as well have been Italian.

She told Matt not to feel guilty that he didn't take her to the doctor four days before she had died. This brought him to tears. He knew she wasn't feeling well, he told me, but she had refused to go. He has been carrying around this self-imposed burden since she had passed.

She also mentioned names that Matt was able to confirm, such as his mother and her husband, and she mentioned Coney Island. She talked about how she used to take him there and tease him about eating Coney Island hotdogs until he was sick. He admitted that he'd became sick after eating just one, but because he loved them so much, he wanted to have as many as she would allow him to buy.

After the reading was over, I was enjoying chatting with people at the party when I was told that Matt had called his mother and his grandfather, both back in New York. His grandmother had asked him to tell them that he had heard from her. I was also told that the one thing which floored Matt was the fact about the Coney Island hot dogs. This was one of his favorite memories of the time he had spent with his grandmother.

My Reading with Anthony
By Tom Bendure

I always considered myself a skeptic and was unsure of my beliefs on how religion works. My wife and I happened to be invited by my sister to a psychic group reading that had been hosted for about three years by two psychic mediums—one of them being Anthony Quinata.

I listened to readings for other people whom I knew and could relate to some of the information they were receiving. At the end of the session, Anthony said that he would get to me soon as a strong presence was pointing my way but that he needed a break.

Anthony walked out of the room, turned and came right back in saying, "She says we have to do this NOW." My mother who had passed about fifteen years prior was coming through. The validation was heightened by way the speech and mannerisms that came through were indeed reminiscent of my mother. The information Anthony imparted was spot on. How was it possible for him to come up with the names of my two hamsters and other types of pets that I had had when growing up? That was unreal and made a believer out of me! The time I have spent in readings and discussions with Anthony has given me cause to re-evaluate in a positive way what I believe about this life and the afterlife! Thank you, Anthony!

* * *

Chapter

16

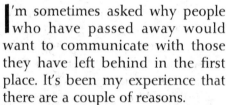

I'm sometimes asked why people who have passed away would want to communicate with those they have left behind in the first place. It's been my experience that there are a couple of reasons.

The first one is love. Their physical bodies have died, but their love for us hasn't. They see our pain and want us to understand that while we're no longer connected physically, they are still connected to us emotionally. The second reason is that they can now see the bigger picture in a way we cannot and want to help us understand that there's a reason for everything which happens here on this physical plane.

A woman named Rena came to see me after her fiancé, Ed, passed away in a tragic accident. During her reading Ed thanked her for the letter she had written to him expressing her feelings after losing him. When the reading was done, she thanked me and left.

A few months later Rena sent me an email with a link to a blog post she had written in which she had blasted me as a fake. Why would Ed communicate with her through me when, while he was alive, he hadn't believed that life continued after death? Shortly before his death, she and Ed had gone to a metaphysical fair where he had expressed his cynicism about the whole thing, and now he was communicating with her through a medium? And how did I know about the letter she had written, and what was written in it? How did I know so much about him? She dismissed it all to nothing more than lucky guesses.

I thought about responding to the post but decided against it. After all, I thought, the souls made it very clear that my responsibility was only to pass the messages along. How they are received is up to the person receiving them.

Almost a year had passed since I had read that post when I was surprised to see Rena again. She sat down in front of me, and I saw tears well up in her eyes. "I'm sorry; I don't want to bother you," she said and got up to leave.

I followed her out to the parking lot and told her, "Before you go, I want a hug." We hugged and I said, "Okay, here's the deal. I'm not letting you go until you tell me why you're here."

She laughed, but when she saw I was serious, she agreed to sit down with me and tell me what was going on. "I really want to apologize for what I wrote about you. I was just so angry and hurt about the reading you gave me. I mean, I couldn't figure out how you knew so much about Ed. The whole thing scared me."

"Well," I told her, "I don't believe that people come to see me unless their loved ones bring them to me, which would explain the real reason you're here. Ed wants to talk to you again." During the last session what had stood out for Rena was the letter. During this session, it was when Ed brought up her collection of turtles. When I mentioned that, Rena lit up.

"He's telling me that you've thought about taking your own life since his passing. Is that true?"

Rena whispered, "Yes."

"He understands that," I told her. "That's why he wanted you to see me the first time and why he inspired you to come and see me today. He doesn't want you to do what you've been thinking about doing."

"I know," she said. "I'm not thinking of doing it anymore. After seeing you before, I realized that I will see Ed again, and if I do commit suicide, then I'd have nothing to show him. I want to live my life the best I can so that when I show him what I've done since he's been gone, he'll be proud of me."

"Well, Ed's not the only one who's proud of you right now," I told her.

My Reading with Anthony
By Jim

I was on a business trip to Denver. My wife came along with me because she had a client there, Cornerstone Books [discussed in Chapters 17, 18, and 19]. I was visiting the store and came in from another room to find my wife speaking with the (former) owner of the store and Anthony. My wife introduced me and said that Anthony speaks with dead people.

Now you have to understand that I come from the bayous of Louisiana where there was all kinds of talk when I was growing up about voodoo and ghosts. So when I heard that Anthony speaks to dead people, I was not sure that I wanted to be in on the conversation.

At one point, Anthony looked at me and asked who the large woman was [to me] and said that she had a loud laugh. I said that it was probably my grandmother. He asked me if she liked to wear hats on Sunday to which I said, "Yes." He was saying how proud she was of me. Okay, so I figured that could have been a good guess.

Then Anthony asked me, "Who is Mabel?" I said that it was Annie Mabel (Auntie Mabel). She had raised my sister in her home while I was raised by my grandparents. Annie Mabel was the cool aunt. She lived in a nice house, had a really cool job, and was fun loving. Anthony said that she thought I was living an exciting life and that she was proud of me, which I knew she was. Annie Mabel told me, as an adult, "Boy, if you die today, the world will owe you nothing."

Okay, now I was starting to get a little concerned that he was able to pull out the uncommon name of Mabel.

Immediately after that, Anthony asked me who Charles was in my life. I said that Charles was my stepfather when I was growing up. Anthony told me that Charles wanted to apologize for how he treated me and that it had had nothing to do with me. It was due to the alcohol that Charles used to numb the pain. This instantly brought tears to my eyes which I had to fight back.

Anthony said that Charles acknowledged that he was not very nice and that he knows how his behavior affected me.

Charles scared me as a kid, especially when he drank. I was really starting to wonder how Anthony could pull out those names and how he would know how I felt about Charles.

Anthony then said that someone was telling him just to say the words "I was in prison," and that I would know who this person was. My uncle Ike had spent three years in Angola for a traffic violation. He raised me from my early teens to adulthood. By this time, I didn't know what was going on.

Then Anthony came straight out and asked me why I never finished school. He said that it was my mother asking the question. This one hit me like a Mack truck. No one other than my mother or my wife knows that I did not finish school. She said that I should finish school. Anthony said that I should make it a point of at least doing this before passing.

Anthony said that she also wanted me to know that she stayed as long as she did with Charles because she felt I needed a father figure.

Anthony then asked if someone close to me had died young. I said it was my younger sister, Margie. Anthony said that she had cancer, to which I said, "Yes." He said that Margie wanted me to tell her kids that she loves them. Anthony told me that Margie forgave the kids for not visiting her and that she wanted me to do the same. She said that the kids were not emotionally capable of visiting her. This subject was a tough one for me because the kids visited her only one time in the thirty days that she was in the hospital. No one, other than my wife, knew that I was angry with my sister's kids for not visiting her more in the hospital.

Halfway through all of this, Anthony had to stop for a minute. He said the gathering on the Other Side was like a cocktail party—there were so many people talking. This was so true of my family. When we all got together, everyone would be talking all at once.

At the end of all of this, I found that I just had to leave because it was all so overwhelming. As my wife and I were driving away, I kept trying to figure out how Anthony would have been able to "guess" two names correctly and come up with the details that he did.

After experiencing this event with Anthony, I believe that he does speak with the dead because there is no way he could have made that such accurate guesses on all the people he spoke of.

* * *

Chapter

17

I decided to start doing small group sessions, and since I wasn't able to do them out of my office, I needed to find some place to hold them. I remembered a little store called Cornerstone Books that had attached to it a conference room which would be perfect for what I needed.

Cornerstone not only had "readers" on a daily basis but also hosted metaphysical events as well, so I thought it would be a perfect fit. I walked into the store and asked for the owner. The woman behind the counter introduced herself as the owner and told me her name was "Deb."

I asked her if the conference room

was available for rent, and she said it was. She told me how much she charged for the room and asked me what I planned to use it for. "Well, I'm a psychic medium, and . . . " I stopped when Deb rolled her eyes.

"Anyway," I continued, "I want to do small group sessions in your conference room." I explained to her that in these sessions I'd do readings for up to twelve people who were hoping to reconnect with their loved ones who had passed away.

She continued to look at me as though I'd lost my mind, and I began to wonder if I had been wrong in thinking that this was the perfect place to hold these sessions. "Well," she finally said after staring at me for a couple of minutes, "Would you mind doing a reading for one of my customers?"

"Not at all," I told her. We talked for a few more minutes as she asked me questions about being a medium. My answers must have convinced her that I wasn't a nut case.

"Would you mind doing a reading for me?" she asked.

"I thought you'd never ask," I told her. I proceeded to give her seven names, and the messages they wanted to pass along to her. She confirmed six of the seven names, one of them being her mother. "Your mother is wagging her finger at you," I told her, shaking my index finger up and down, "and telling you to pay your taxes."

"Tell her I'm trying!" she told me, her voice rose slightly. "I can't believe it. My mother has been dead for eighteen years now, and she's still wagging her finger at me." We talked for a few more minutes, and she said, "Well, come back Monday afternoon, and I'll have a couple of keys made for you so you can get into the conference room." With that, she walked away.

I got the impression that she was less than impressed with the reading I gave her even though I thought it had gone well. I even wondered whether I should come back because I didn't know if she'd change her mind about making keys for me.

I decided to take a chance and went back to the store the following Monday. This time there was a young man named Sean behind the counter. "Hi," I said, "Is Deb here?"

"No, she's not." Turns out I was right after all I thought to myself. "May I help you with something?" he asked.

"Well, I was here couple of days ago hoping to be able to rent the conference room," not knowing why I was even bothering. "I did a reading for her, and she told me to come by today to pick up keys."

Sean lit up and said, "Oh! You must be Anthony!"

"You know who I am?" I asked, stunned.

"You bet! Deb has been raving about you to everyone here and everyone who's been coming into the store! She says you're amazing!"

Wow, the woman who rolled her eyes at me and then acted so nonchalant after I read her was raving about me! I didn't know whether or not to believe that, but she must have been doing so, because when I had my first small group session at the store two weeks later, it was full. And I didn't do any marketing.

The second small group session I did at Cornerstone was also full. When people showed up, they didn't have to make an appointment to attend. All they had to do was show up and pay the fee to be a part of the group. Once they were there, they were instructed not to talk to anyone, even the other people attending, about whom they were hoping to reconnect with. If they did, they'd be asked to leave.

They didn't even have to introduce themselves to anyone. All I asked that they do was show up with an open mind.

The dynamics of a group session of any size is much different from a one-on-one session or even a family session where there may be two or more people. A private session, even a family session, is a little like a dinner conversation, whereas a group session is like a cocktail party and everyone there wants my attention. I also ask the souls to stay by their loved ones until I get there, and that's when they remind me I'm not always the one in charge.

During one of these sessions I was talking to an elderly mother and her daughter. "There's a man standing next to you," I told the mother, and he says his name is George. He's not telling me how he's related to you, so I'm assuming he's your husband."

Anger flashed across her face, and she said, "My husband's name isn't George." I could tell by the look on her face that this just proved what she believed all along—I'm a fake, and this was a waste of her time.

I became aware that there was a woman with "George," and when I asked her what her name was, I saw the Book of Alma from the Book of Mormon. "Do you know who Alma is? She's with George."

"I don't know who that is either," she answered, her face becoming even more set.

Was I discerning the information I was receiving incorrectly? I never claimed to be 100 percent accurate, but I was sure I was right, or at least close on this. Going on the whole Book of Mormon image, I tried again, "Are you Mormon?"

"No." I could tell that she was now ready to get up and leave.

"Do you mind if I come back to you?" Her daughter put her hand on her mother's shoulder. Since she continued to sit there, I took that as a "yes."

Twenty minutes later, one of the women at the session said to me, "Anthony, when you were talking to them," she nodded her head at the mother and daughter, "you mentioned you were connected to a George and Alma."

"Do you know who they are?" I asked.

"Well," she said, hesitantly, "my grandfather was George, and my grandmother was Alta."

"Why didn't you say something?" I asked.

"You were talking to them, and I didn't want to interrupt!" she said sheepishly.

After bringing this lady's grandfather and grandmother for her, I went back to the mother and daughter and brought through the mother's husband. As she listened to what I had to say, the look on her face went from anger to disbelief. Eventually she finally started smiling and thanked me for the reading.

All's well that ends well.

My Reading with Anthony
By Deb Guinther
(former owner of Cornerstone Books, Englewood, Colorado)

It has been six years since Anthony Quinata walked into Cornerstone Books inquiring about renting the meeting room to do psychic readings for people who have experienced loss. I think he said that he "communicated with the dead!"

After fifteen years of many EXPERTS who had come to me, selling their talents, I had my guard up with Anthony. As soon as he said he talked with the dead, I rolled my eyes and thought that here we go again with another expert in the psychic reader, intuitive category! His charm, experience, and enthusiasm for how he could bring more business to the store captured my attention, and I decided to give him a little of my time.

We took care of the details around renting the room and scheduled an evening where he would facilitate small groups whose members wanted to get in touch with their loved ones who had transitioned. We concluded by discussing content and group format for his workshop.

By now Anthony had raised my curiosity enough that I asked him how he had gotten into the field and cultivated the "talent!" Anthony explained that he had resisted the "calling" for many years, and then friends convinced him that he had a responsibility to pursue this phenomenon. The reason I say phenomenon is that I still wasn't 100 percent convinced that anyone could have this gift, let alone Anthony, who was standing right in front of me!

Then all of a sudden Anthony said, "Oh wait, someone is coming through, and she wants me to tell you . . . " That someone was my aunt, and once Anthony described her personality, gave me her name, and said that she was the dominating voice at the family gathering, he now had my attention. The time flew by and for an hour I had had my mouth hanging open and goose bumps on my arms. I thought that I had come very close to having to eat crow and to make amends for my "doubting Thomas" attitude and rudeness.

In that hour Anthony had mentioned every family member by name, told how they had died, and described each one with specific characteristics and messages that carried meaning only for me. When my mother came, Anthony asked if she had wagged her finger a lot and was strict as well as loving. The relatives were at a gathering, all talking at the same time, and Anthony was having trouble hearing them individually. The detail was remarkable, and in one hour I was a believer in his work.

Once Anthony started the small group sessions, I began to receive phone calls and notes from those who had attended. The comments included not only the moving experiences they had had but also the healing and forgiveness opportunities he had offered. To this day, the ultimate compliment was that Anthony's sessions were the best service we had ever offered.

Yes, I am a reformed skeptic, and I am thrilled that Anthony's work will be available to those who want the personal healing experience of hearing from the departed.

Blessings to my dear friend Anthony Quinata!

*   *   *

Chapter

18

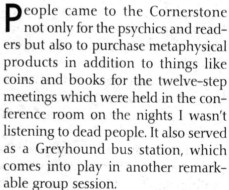

People came to the Cornerstone not only for the psychics and readers but also to purchase metaphysical products in addition to things like coins and books for the twelve-step meetings which were held in the conference room on the nights I wasn't listening to dead people. It also served as a Greyhound bus station, which comes into play in another remarkable group session.

It was a full session with twelve people, and as usual, I wanted to make sure everyone who was there received a reading. Two of my friends, Rachel and Miguel, are videographers and were filming the session that night.

Thirty minutes before everyone was supposed to arrive, I was telling Rachel that someone was coming to reconnect with a person who had committed suicide. "How do you know," she asked me.

"Because I can feel the energy of the person who did it, and it's as heavy as it gets."

When people started arriving, they were told that the session that night would be videotaped. They were also asked, if they were going to stay, to sign release forms. I gave Rachel and Miguel permission to break my usual protocol by asking for their names and phone numbers on the forms.

When the session began, I said, "One of you is here to reconnect with someone who committed suicide." The only male, other than Miguel, there that night raised his hand. Rachel looked at me shocked.

"I'm getting that she is a female who was very close to you when she was still here." He nodded, tears starting to fill his eyes. "Well, she's really anxious to talk to you, but I'm asking her to wait until I explain how tonight is going to work."

I explained what everyone could expect from the session, gave him his reading, and moved on to read everyone else there. The chairs were arranged in a semicircle to make the session easier to film. The last person to receive a reading was an attractive young woman, twenty years old, whose expression said that she was becoming impatient waiting for her reading. Well, she was going to have to wait a little longer, but neither she nor I knew why at that time.

"I'm with you now," I told her. "I want to thank you for being so patient and waiting. I have a woman claiming to be your grandmother standing behind you. I want to say her name is Maria."

"Both of my grandmothers are still alive," she told me.

"Is her name Maria?" I asked.

"No."

"Oh boy," I thought, "the night was going so well up until now! And if that wasn't enough, this is being videotaped!"

"Well, who's Victor?" I asked. "She keeps saying the name Victor."

"I don't know who Victor is."

"He's seventeen, a senior in high school, and plays soccer. I'm being told he's really good at it," giving the information I was getting. "Is Victor your boyfriend?"

"I told you; I don't know who Victor is," she said angrily. "Besides, I'm twenty years old, and I would not have a boyfriend who is only seventeen and still in high school."

I might be talking to the wrong person, I thought to myself. "Is there anyone here who can claim this?" I asked looking around. That's when I noticed a little face looking at us through one of the windows of the conference room.

"Would someone mind looking outside and telling me if there's someone out there who looks like he's waiting on a bus?"

The guy who had earlier connected with his ex-girlfriend who had committed suicide jumped up. "I'll go check," he said, walking out the door. A moment later he came back in. "There are people out there. There's a teenager, a woman, and a little boy."

"Would you mind telling them what's going on here and ask them to come in?" I requested. He smiled and left the store again. "Wouldn't you like to be listening in on that conversation? There's a guy in here that's talking to dead people and wants to talk to you." Everyone laughed along with me.

"Here they are," my messenger said, walking back in the store.

A young Hispanic teenager around high-school age came into the conference room, followed by someone whom I assumed was his sister, who appeared to be a couple of years older, and a little boy; the same boy I had seen looking in the window.

"I'm helping these people reconnect with their loved ones who have passed away," I explained to him, "and I think I have someone here who wants to talk to you. Are you Victor?"

He nodded his head nervously. "How do you know my name?"

"I'll tell you in a minute, but first I need to confirm a couple of things. Are you seventeen?"

He looked at his sister who looked just as nervous as he did. "Yes."

"Are you a senior in high school?"

"Yes."

"Who's Maria to you?"

"Mara," he corrected me, "my grandmother."

"She's passed away," I said.

"Yes."

"Well, the only way to explain this to you is that Mara, your grandmother, has a message or two for you. You play soccer. Yes?"

"Yes."

"Your grandmother tells me you have dreams of becoming a professional," I continued.

That's right," he said, smiling.

"Well, she's telling me that you're good enough to make that dream happen." Now he was smiling from ear to ear, beaming with pride. "She's also telling me that you drank tequila for the first time the other night."

Victor held his index finger and thumb apart to show that he didn't drink that much. "I don't care how much or how little you drank to be honest with you, but she says that you swallowed the worm."

Victor and his sister looked at each other with their mouths hanging open. "Your grandmother says you've also started drinking beer lately, a lot of beer. She's concerned that if you keep this up, you'll not only ruin your chances of becoming a professional soccer player, but your chances of getting a scholarship into a good school as well."

Victor's cocky attitude suddenly changed into one of embarrassment. "Tell her I'll stop."

"You just did," I told him. I looked at his sister, "Your grandmother wants me to tell you she loves you and your son, but she really wanted to scold your brother." We all laughed at that.

Victor and his sister thanked me and left to wait for Victor's bus. As soon as the door closed behind them, I returned to the young lady whose reading had been interrupted and began by saying, "You're here to connect with a young woman, a cousin around your age. Is that right?"

She nodded.

"Good. Well she's telling me . . . " As I talked, I realized that the bench where people sat waiting for the bus was directly behind her from where I was sitting.

My Reading with Anthony

By Gina Alianello

In all the years since my parents died, it never occurred to me to see a medium. I had heard about Anthony one day when I was shopping in a bookstore. Anthony was going to be doing a small group session at the store, and the shop owner raved about him. Still, the idea of seeing a medium seemed more novel than real.

At age forty five, I was the proverbial "orphan" who never grew up, forever confounded at my lost confidence. After experiencing many personal breakthroughs with energy healing methods that I had discovered in my quest to get better from an auto accident, I began feeling proud of myself, determined that I was through wallowing in self-pity and that I was moving on from everyone—living and dead as well as the old images of a Catholic God that didn't make sense to me anymore.

I decided to take a chance and attend one of Anthony's group sessions, hoping to hear anything that might heal my loneliness and hurt. What I got was more than I could have ever hoped for.

Although he didn't know it at the time, my sister-in-law, Cathy, agreed to go with me. When Anthony began his reading for me, he said he noticed my mother standing between my sister-in-law and me and that she was there for both of us. He said my mother was standing next to Mother Mary and that she was holding rosary beads. For two years before she had died, my mom had become deeply devoted to Mary and the rosary through the well-known apparitions in Yugoslavia.

Anthony told me that my mother was saying "it wouldn't hurt" for me to say the rosary—words she had often used throughout my life to urge me to do things I resisted. I could hardly believe it. After so many blurry years without her, here was my mother picking up with me as if she had never been gone—and just when I had finally determined praying the rosary was not for me, despite how I had shared in her devotion and had turned to the rosary after she died. But now I groaned, twisted in my seat, and complained how I did not want to say the rosary. Anthony ex-

103

plained to the group that the Other Side is not necessarily Catholic, but the rosary is a powerful prayer often requested by those who have died.

Anthony continued by saying that he saw a crowd of my relatives all talking and kidding around. I thought of the warmth and exuberance of so many around my parents when they had been alive. Anthony talked about my mom, dad, uncle, and others describing exactly how they had died.

Then Anthony said, "Charlie wants to say 'hi' to Bob." I had called my grandpa Charlie, and Bob was now his only living son and my father's only living sibling. I shrieked with delight. Anthony said, of all things, that "they" were congratulating me on getting a new car. It seemed so incidental or trivial that "they" would bring up the car—yet I had spent the summer by myself trying to find the first decent car of my life on a tiny budget. Car trouble had been a running joke in our family with my father's string of unreliable heaps. This car purchase had been symbolic of overcoming my years of stress in dilapidated cars, being embarrassed and scared as I had barely made it from job to job.

Anthony went on to say that my parents wanted to know why I wasn't singing anymore. I was sure Anthony had it wrong; I was an aspiring writer, not a singer. But in two other later sessions, he repeated this and insisted they were telling me to sing. My mother was saying that singing was healing for me as it had been for my father. She named "Caruso" whose operatic voice my father had loved. I pictured how my dad always sang to the old-time tunes on the radio with a gleam in his eyes.

Months later, I caught myself singing full force to the radio, as I had not done since I was younger when I had last felt confident and alive. Such a small thing suddenly made sense. As a girl in my bedroom next to my parents' room, I had practiced and choreographed singing as loud as I could to the radio and stereo, pretending to be a famous star. I hadn't realized how much they saw. Riding in the car with my mom, I had always sung every word to every hit on the radio, providing earnest commentary between each song.

Anthony told me that my father said he is with me when I drink my tea. That means my father has been with me a lot, because over the years my teacup has been like an appendage, getting me through so my times alone as I've struggled through chronic grief and sickness. It seemed so insignificant when he said it. I wondered why my parents seemed so intent on telling me such minor details. Now as time passes, I realize it was their way of telling me that they are still with me and watching over me. They, just like God, love me in the small, seemingly inconsequential details of my life.

My image of God has changed to something more merciful, creative, and personal than I could have imagined. After the readings, I cried—no, I poured out tears for hours every day for several months. I began to wonder if I would ever stop. I was still healing from my car accident at the time, but my tears seemed to come from some unceasing pool of profound relief and wonder, most often beyond my apprehension. I am still processing my new reality, still sometimes gripped by the mystery of grief and death, but my heart knows a comfort it never knew before and a confidence that the love which matters never ends. I have a new and deeper attachment to those who have gone on and I pray for them, happy and overwhelmed to know we all still need each other.

I thank God for bringing Anthony into my life. Now when I hear a song on the radio that especially reminds me of my parents, I know they really hear me and that they're near. Sometimes, I even sing.

*   *   *

Chapter

19

As I said before, there wasn't a requirement that people who wanted a reading in a small group session at Cornerstone had to sign up in advance or let me know that they were coming. Occasionally, though, I did know who would be there beforehand. Trish was one of those occasions.

She had called a week before wanting to book an appointment with me for a one-on-one reading. She told me that she had heard about me from friends of hers who had had readings from me. "I'm a scientist," she told me. "I'm also the mother of two little boys, six and four. Science teaches, and I believed, that when someone dies, that's it. It's over. Now that I'm a mother, I can't bring myself to accept that."

I suggested that rather than a one-on-one reading, she should attend one of my group sessions. "That way you can observe other people being read as well. I'll save your reading for last." She agreed and even sounded excited about the idea of seeing me read other people.

The night of the group reading I introduced her and why she was there. I also asked her to repeat to them what she had told me over the phone. "As a scientist fully aware of the nature of science, I know that there are always going to be more questions than answers; there are areas that the laws of science just can't adequately explain, if at all. Yet, this doesn't always mean that they don't exist or aren't real. Personally, I would like to explore this further to see what this is all about."

As the night went on and she saw other people being read, the look on her face went from being guarded to bewilderment. After one reading with a woman who had lost her boyfriend when he had crashed after having fallen asleep behind the wheel of his car in the mountains as he was coming home from work, I noticed that she was crying along with everyone else there. I asked her if she was okay.

"This wasn't what I was expecting," she told me. "I came here thinking I'd hear you throwing out vague generalities that people would fill in, but you're so specific with what you're saying. I don't know what to think right now."

"Well, it's your turn. Are you ready?" I asked. She nodded. "Okay, just answer yes or no to whatever I say. You're here to reconnect with a female. Yes?"

She looked at me, wide-eyed, and nodded her head. "Yes," she said.

Psychically I felt as though my body was being slammed, and I felt a sharp pain in my neck, so I started to rub it. "I'm feeling an impact, and my neck is hurting. The pain in my neck is sharp, so sharp that it's making me want to wince. I want to say that this person was in a car accident and either gets whiplash or a broken neck. I want to go with the broken neck. She passes from a broken neck. Yes?"

Trish confirmed what I was saying by nodding. She started crying again.

"This woman is coming across as older than you. No offense, but she's kind of pushy," I told Trish. I smiled at her to let her know I was okay with this.

"That definitely sounds like her!" Trish started laughing, which caused all of us to laugh.

"Even though she's older than you, she makes me feel as though you two were close," I continued. "Does this make sense?"

"Yes."

"She's making me feel as though she's your sister, but I want to say she was a cousin of yours," I offered.

"She was my cousin, but we were more like sisters," Trish told me sniffling.

I continued to pass on the impressions I was receiving. "She's telling me that she has two children, a boy and a girl. The girl is with her in spirit. Do you understand what she's telling me?"

"Yes." Trish began crying harder.

"I want to say that this girl passes young, not young as in a miscarriage or abortion, or as an infant. She's a young girl when she passes. Does this make sense?"

"Did you and your cousin go to Disneyland together?" I asked Trish.

"No," she shook her head.

"Huh. I asked that because she's showing me Mickey Mouse, and I always associate Mickey Mouse with Disneyland. I thought your families went to Disneyland because I'm seeing Mickey Mouse. You must have gone to Sea World in San Diego together then."

Trish's eyes became wide. "We did go to Sea World together, but not to Disneyland."

"Okay, because I'm seeing Shamu, the killer whale," I said to explain how I came to that conclusion. "I saw Shamu when I was a kid and my family went to Sea World." The memory made me smile.

"Hmmm, why is she showing me Mickey Mouse again?" I wondered out loud. Then a map of Florida appeared (psychically) in front of me. Everything started to fall into place for me. "Was your cousin vacationing in Florida when she passed?"

Trish looked at me stunned. "Yes."

"Okay, because I'm seeing Mickey Mouse. I'm hearing the sickening sound of metal against metal, and my neck feels as though my head is being whipped to the right." Suddenly what I was seeing, feeling, and hearing, all became clear to me. "Your cousin was vacationing in Florida when she passed away. They were there to go to Disneyworld. The car she was in was hit by another car that ran a red light."

Trish nodded confirming everything I just said. She was covering her face with a tissue and crying hard causing her shoulders to go up and down. We all could hear her sobbing, so I waited before I continued.

"Are you getting anything else?" she whispered. I nodded. "Go on," she said.

"She's telling me that her daughter was in the car with her when the accident happened. Her daughter passed away from her injuries as well, but not right away. Your cousin was there to cross her over, but she had to wait a little while in order to do so."

Trish confirmed what I was saying for everyone at the session. "She and her daughter were in the back seat when they were hit by another car. It hit them right where my cousin was sitting. Her daughter didn't die right away. She died a few hours later."

"Was her daughter a ballerina?" I asked. "I see her wearing a tutu. I'm being told that she was taking ballet dancing lessons. Yes?" Without waiting for an answer, I continued. "Her daughter's telling me that she's dancing for Jesus now. Your cousin's husband is remarried." This time I looked at her and waited for an answer.

"Yes."

"He has children with his new wife."

"Yes."

"Your cousin wants him to know that she's happy he has

moved on with his life. She's happy he married again. She's especially happy that their son has a new brother and sister."

Trish looked at me astonished. I thought she was going to jump out of her seat as she said, almost in a shout, "OH MY GOD! He does have a boy and a girl with his new wife!"

"This is her way of letting her husband know that she's still with him and her son. Please tell them that you heard from your cousin and their daughter and that they both send their love." I started to feel their energy pulling away. "They're being called back now, but your cousin thanks you for having the courage to do this. She sends her love to you. And they're gone."

The people who were at the session that night quietly cried along with Trish, but all of their eyes were bright with hope. "I want to thank all of you for being here tonight and for being open to the souls who came through for you. Any questions before we end tonight?" I asked. "Trish?"

"That's just it! I have more questions now than I did before I came here!"

I know the feeling. I've been doing this for several years now, and I still have more questions than answers. But the answers I do have and what I've learned from the souls, I'd like to share with you in the rest of this book.

Chapter

20

Before I started doing this work, I used to wear a T-shirt that said, "It's not that life is so short. It's just that death is so long!"

One of the things I've heard over and over again from the souls is that the way we think of death is simply incorrect. It's not a wall that separates us. It's more like a door through which we go from one room into another. While the experience is not the same for everyone, the process essentially is.

There's a moment of complete darkness, almost like falling asleep. If the person were in any pain, all suffering ceases immediately and so does any fear, anger, or resentments that may have existed.

Soon a light appears in the darkness, and the soul starts to move towards it. As the soul moves closer and deeper into the light, it begins to see loved ones who have died before. Beloved pets that have passed away are seen as well. Many souls have said that it is at this moment in the midst of the joy of seeing their loved ones when the realization hits them that they, too, have died.

Of course, not everyone is ready to make the transition. The passing may have been sudden, tragic, and unexpected—the results of a car crash, heart attack, or murder. These souls may cross over feeling, "Whoa! This isn't fair! It wasn't my time to go!" Souls, such as these, are welcomed with patience, love, and understanding by God and the spirits already on the Other Side. These newly arrived souls are also encouraged to rest and are given space to adjust to their new lives.

Then there are those souls who, when they were living in this plane of existence, didn't believe in an afterlife. I remember seeing a woman whose husband had been an atheist when he had died. I didn't know this, so when he told me to tell his wife that she had won the bet, I didn't know what he was talking about.

She laughed. "I'm a Christian. He didn't believe in God or a life after death. He believed that once you died, that was it—end of story. We had a wager. I bet him that when he died, he would find out I was right all along."

Her husband had suffered from lung cancer for years, and one night he fell asleep and didn't wake up. "I felt really good," he told me. "In fact, I felt better than I had in years. My lungs didn't hurt anymore. Then I saw my old hunting dog. He kept barking and wanted me to follow him, so I did. I saw my mother and father who had died years ago. I saw my younger brother who had died years before. I thought I was a dreaming. I figured that eventually I'd just wake up and be in pain again. My parents and brother helped me understand that I wasn't dreaming. I had died. I always thought that when people died, they wouldn't even know that they were ever alive, but I'm still alive. In fact, I'm more alive than I was when I was alive! I don't know how else to explain it. I'm still not sure I believe what's going on."

Whether it's because of the suddenness of their passing or a disbelief in the afterlife, souls that are unable to accept the reality of their new life are given a chance to adjust and come to terms with their new reality. This is essentially a time of healing, a time to "rest in peace."

There are souls who don't need this "time out," but because this is such a new experience, in order to make the transition easier to navigate, I've been told that experiences in this life serve as points of reference while making the adjustment. For example, Camille's father, Tom, loved ice cream when he was here on this plane of existence. During Camille's reading her father talked about having an ice cream stand. It gave him a tremendous amount of joy to serve a cone to everyone who wanted ice cream, but most especially to children.

Another friend, and colleague of mine, the late Natalie Smith-Blakeslee received a reading from me in which her daughter, Carrie, came through. Carrie had passed from leukemia at a young age. While she was still here, she loved swimming and children. During Natalie's session with me, Carrie proudly told her mother that she was teaching children how to swim on the Other Side.

One of the more amazing things I've learned is that we can also choose the life we wanted to live here on earth, but for whatever reason, we were not able to do so. Whatever we wanted in this life is available for us in the next and is ours for as long as we need it. When we're able to release these desires in exchange for a deeper relationship with God, we become more open to even more of the joy, happiness, and peace that come with this deepened relationship.

Chapter

21

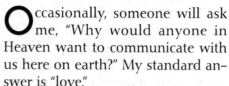

Occasionally, someone will ask me, "Why would anyone in Heaven want to communicate with us here on earth?" My standard answer is "love."

It's only natural to want to share with the people we care about something we've learned or discovered which we think they might benefit from: a good movie, restaurant, recipe, mechanic, etc. The desire to share what's important and helpful seems to be even more so for those who have crossed over and have gone through their life review.

All souls go through a review of their life here on earth. They are made aware of how their life, actions, and attitudes had an impact on the lives of those they loved and others. They are shown the ways that they were helpful and harmful, sometimes without them even knowing it. They begin to understand the effects of their actions from the point of view of those affected.

This review is done in the presence of God, but this isn't a time of judgment. The souls have told me it's the exact opposite—God is very compassionate and nonjudgmental and holds them in love.

One day I was thinking about what I've been told about the life review process and the love the souls experience during this time. I prayed and asked to be able to experience what this felt like, and I was immediately given, symbolically, an idea of what this was like. The experience is almost indescribable. I felt like a grain of sand in the middle of an ocean. Everywhere I looked, for as far as I could see, I was not only surrounded, but also supported and protected by this water, which symbolized the love souls experience during their life review.

The souls have also told me that all of their questions about their lives are answered during this time. They learn the reasons for all of their lives' mishaps and misfortunes. Any and all suffering we've endured makes sense and is rewarded. I've heard countless number of times from the souls that they would gladly have endured even more suffering than they had, say during a terminal disease, if they had known what awaited them for having experienced it.

Our souls were created in love. We came here to learn lessons in love. The growth of our spirit is easier due to the people and experiences we have encountered while we're here. All of the circumstances that happened while we are here are for our own good and our process of developing and maturing spiritually. If we have spent our time here wisely, staying close to our life's purpose, then we are able to place ourselves on a level that is closer to God.

Souls are also made aware of opportunities that were squandered. If people lived their lives here hurting others and wasting their opportunities to grow spiritually, they see, during their life review, how their foolish behavior affected everyone around them. The pain brought on by the realization of their lack of love causes them to place themselves in a level that is farther away from God.

Every once in a while, whenever I talk about the lack of judgment on God's part during and after the life review, the subject of "hell" and eternal punishment comes up. I can tell you only what I've been told by the souls whom I've asked about the subject.

It doesn't exist.

That doesn't mean that we have a free pass to do whatever pleases us at the expense of others. The souls have told me that no one escapes responsibility for the hurt and suffering we've caused others, but it isn't God who holds us accountable. We hold ourselves responsible when we come to understand, first-hand, how what we did, or didn't do, hurt others and stunted our own spiritual growth. When you're surrounded by the love that permeates everything on the Other Side, love becomes the benchmark by which you'll judge your actions in this life.

After I wrote the last paragraph, the souls gave me a symbol that makes sense to me, and I hope it will make sense to you as well. What they showed me was a light bulb that was connected to a "dimmer switch." The bulb is like our souls, and the switch is our lives.

The way we live our lives determines how bright or how dim our souls appear after our life review. The better we do here as far living our life's purpose, the brighter we are. If we spend our lives wreaking havoc not only in our life but also in the lives of others, the dimmer our light is on the Other Side.

We choose how bright or dim our light shines by our love and our actions—the way we treat ourselves and others.

I cannot stress enough what I've been told by the souls and that is the fact that no one is lost to God. There is nothing anyone can do that could cause him/her to be unlovable as far as God is concerned. There is always some light, some love that shines in every soul, and every soul wants to be loved.

No people's light is ever entirely extinguished to the point that God doesn't "see" or love them. If they're not lost to God, they are not lost to you.

After their life review, souls will continue their journey of spiritual development to learn the lessons they missed here. They are given opportunities to repair the damage caused while they were here on earth. Part of that journey is to guide us on ours while we're still here. The wisdom souls acquire during their life review is what they want to impart to those they have left behind. Their desire to share what they've learned with us is immense, if we'd only listen.

I was working at a psychic fair when Sarah, an astrologer, walked up to me. "I have a question to ask you," she said. "I was told recently that my late father-in-law is still with me and I was wondering if it's true."

"It is, and it isn't." I told her. "He's keeping his distance out of respect for you. He's telling me that you two didn't get along. Is that true?"

"Yeah," Sarah admitted.

"He's telling me he wasn't easy to get along with. Anyway, he does want me to pass a message on to you. He says, 'I'm sorry.'"

"Oh, now you're going to make me cry!" Sarah said. I could see tears in her eyes, which surprised me. I continued passing on the messages I was getting.

"He's telling me you helped take care of him for a long time. I mean a long time."

"Twenty years," she said.

"He's making me feel as though he had some sort of disability. Something he was born with, but it was more of a mental disability, than a physical one," I continued.

"He had Asperger's," she told me.

"I'm sorry. He had what?" I asked.

"Asperger's, it's a form of autism," she explained.

"Oh, okay. Did you feed him? He's showing me you had to feed him."

"Yes, I did," she said. "I changed his diapers too!"

"Well, he didn't show me that, thank God!" I said, laughing. "He is telling me that he felt entitled to all the care you gave him. He's saying he feels differently since his 'life review', and now he's grateful for all that you've done for him. He keeps saying that he's sorry. He hopes you'll forgive him."

"I can do that," Sarah said sniffling.

"Please pray for him too."

Sarah nodded. "All I wanted to know was whether or not he was still with me. I wasn't expecting this. I really wasn't expecting an apology. I didn't think that people had a change of heart once they crossed over."

"When a soul crosses over, everything is seen more clearly during the life review," I told her. "I call the life review 'the answer sheet to all of life's questions.' During his review he saw how hard this was for you and how you did this out of love, not because he was entitled. That's why he's asking for your forgiveness. It's absolutely necessary not only for his spiritual advancement on the Other Side but also for your own spiritual growth here. I realize that after twenty years of putting up with him, it may not be the easiest thing to do, but it's the best thing you can do—for his journey on the Other Side and for yours in this life."

Sarah nodded and walked away. Later, as she was leaving the fair, she walked up to me and gave me a hug—something she had never done before in all the years I've known her. Healing came that day to two lives on both sides of the veil.

Chapter

22

In order for communication between the souls and their loved ones to happen, there has to be at least two people. One of them has to be someone who has died and crossed over to the Other Side and who wants to communicate with someone left behind. The second person is someone who wants, or at least is willing, to receive the messages and acknowledge their importance and meaning.

Souls can start communicating with their loved ones they've left behind almost as soon as they cross over. Often they'll do so just to let us know that they're okay and no longer in pain.

The first time I had dinner with Joey (whom I talked about in the Introduction) and his wife, I asked him, "Who's Frank?"

"Who's Frank?" he repeated. "Is this someone who has died?"

"I'm assuming so," I told him.

"I don't know a Frank who has died," Joey said, starting to look a little worried. Keep in mind that he's from Guam and not at all comfortable with this sort of thing. When I asked him if I could bring a friend with me for dinner, he was worried no one else would be able to see my "friend."

"Okay," I said. "Then who do you know by the name of Fran."

He shook his head and said, "No one."

"Well, then," I pressed on, "who do you know with the 'F' name, but I really want to say, 'Frank.'"

"I'm telling you," Joey insisted, "I don't know anyone by the name of Frank who has died. My best friend is named Frank, but he's still alive!"

I decided to let it go. I thanked Joey and his wife, Sue, for the great meal and left.

The next day Joey received a phone call from his mother to let him know that his best friend, Frank, had died the day before. Joey asked me what Frank had wanted to say. I told him that I didn't know since the communication didn't get that far.

You don't have to be a medium in order to experience your loved ones communicating with you from beyond the veil. When loved ones pass away, they will communicate with you in small ways to let you know that they're still around. It might be a thought that comes into your head out of nowhere that makes you think of your loved one. It may be familiar scent such as the cologne or perfume they wore when they were still with you.

Dreams are one of the most common ways that our loved ones let us know that they're still with us. When a loved one visits you in a dream, it seems more real than a typical dream. It's more vivid and memorable. The experience stays with long after you wake up.

Brad, whom I had met several years ago, told me about his sister, who was born with a number of physical disabilities. She had to wear leg braces, which caused her to have, what he called, "a Frankenstein walk." She also had severe asthma attacks and epileptic seizures.

One night, when Brad was still in his teens, his sister started seizing and having an asthma attack. The episode was so severe that her parents called for paramedics who immediately decided she had to go to the hospital. Brad's mother and father told Brad and his brother to stay home. They told them that they would call later and let them know how she was doing.

Since this wasn't his sister's first trip to the hospital, Brad wasn't too worried, so he went to bed and fell asleep. He had a dream in which he saw his sister no longer doing her "Frankenstein walk," but running in a meadow with a large, beautiful smile on her face. He woke up and knew she had died. A moment later the phone rang, confirming what he already knew.

Souls are energy, so one of the easiest ways for them to let us know that they're around is with electricity. One of my favorite stories along these lines happened to a friend of mine named Traci. Traci's parents had a stove with a digital clock that had stopped working. Her father was a scientist and a handyman, and he became more and more frustrated when he couldn't fix the clock. His frustration and constant muttering about the clock grew to the point that it had become a joke between Traci and her mother.

Traci's father died from a sudden heart attack. He died without fixing the clock he had vowed to his wife he would fix. After Traci and her mother got home from the burial, Traci noticed something that made her scream for her mother. The clock, which her father couldn't fix for more than two years, was working perfectly. "Do you think that my father fixed the clock?" Traci asked me later.

"Well," I said, "he did promise your mother that one way or another he would fix the damned thing!" I think he killed two birds with one stone. He made the repair, and let them know he was still around.

Flickering lights are another way they'll let us know that we aren't alone or forgotten. I remember one reading in which Chrissie, a young girl who had taken her life when she was only fifteen years old, told her mother to cancel the appointment her father had made with the electrician. The lights going on and off the way they were for the past week were her way of having fun with them. Kathie, Chrissie's mother, told me that her husband had become so frustrated at what the lights were doing that he had made an appointment for someone to come out and look at them just the day before. We both got a kick out of that one.

Music is another way that our loved ones reach out to us. How do you know if a song is a contact from the Other Side? I think one of the most common ways is that a thought someone who has passed away will suddenly pop into your head and at almost the same time a song, which reminds you of the person, comes on the radio.

One day I had an appointment at my home office to do a reading for a woman. I had a few minutes between my last appointment and hers, so I turned the radio on in my family room to help me relax. I heard a knock on my door. I opened it and invited her in. As soon as she walked in the door, she burst into tears. "How did you know?" she asked me.

"I'm sorry," I replied. "How did I know what?"

"That this is my husband's and my favorite song? How did you know to play it when I came here?"

Of course, I had no idea. Was it just a coincidence? Personally, I don't think it was and neither did she. Not for a moment. We both thought it was her husband's way of saying "hello."

Smells are another form of communication from our loved ones who have crossed over. I was doing a reading for a woman who had lost her father. At one point, we could both smell cigar smoke. Her father, she told me, loved to smoke cigars. At the end of the session, we smelled a man's cologne. She told me that she'd recognize the smell anywhere. It was the cologne her father had worn every day until he became ill.

Denise, whose daughter Jasmine took her own life, contacted me to ask if I thought Jasmine was trying to communicate with her. One of Jasmine's favorite things to do was to draw hearts everywhere. It was sort of her personal "signature."

One day, after a snow storm, Denise walked out to her car to see a perfectly drawn heart in the snow on the hood of her car. She sent me a picture of the heart. It took my breath away and sent chills up and down my spine. "Do you think it was Jasmine?" she asked me.

"I'm sure it was," I told Denise.

I could go on talking about how our loved ones reach out to us but rather than doing that, I'd like to caution you against becoming dependent on "signs" from your loved ones. There's a danger that rather than using them to move through your grief, you may become stuck instead. In other words, not receiving signs does not mean that you're not loved. It may mean just the opposite.

If there's one message that those on the Other Side want us to hear more than any other, it's that they have not abandoned us. They will always be with us, especially when we can use their guidance. Just don't make it a "full-time job" for them.

As I said at the beginning of this chapter, you have to be open to receiving messages and accepting them when they come. Most of the time, these attempts at communication from the souls are dismissed as flukes or coincidences. It's been my experience that when this happens often enough, the souls will inspire their loved ones to contact someone like me.

Chapter

23

Many people think that when I'm communicating with someone who is on the Other Side, I'm having a conversation with the soul. I wish it were as simple as, "Hi, it's me, your daughter Patty, the one who thought she'd live forever, but found out differently when she hit that telephone pole with her car because she was texting on her phone and not paying attention while she was driving. I just want you to know that I'm doing great, and I'm still with you. Please give my brother Vince a hug for me. Say hi to Grandma and Grandpa. I love you all."

In all actuality it may be just that simple, but then the souls run into a problem—me. The beautiful messages they send come into my brain and start bouncing around like the metal ball in a pinball machine, and when they finally come out of my mouth . . . well, by that time we're hoping for the best.

The way I receive messages during a reading is through sounds, images, feelings, and thoughts that are conveyed to me through my five "psychic" senses:

Clairsentience (clear sensing)—Typically during a reading, this is how I first discern the presence of soul. I sense it. During the reading this is how a soul will let me know emotions it has felt or is feeling. The soul may also use this method to let me know how it transitioned from this life into the next.

For example, if someone crossed over due to a heart attack, I've felt as though I'm having a heart attack. If the person had COPD or another lung disease, I'll have trouble breathing. If the life ended by suicide, I'll feel extremely depressed. If the person was murdered, I'll feel a sharp, stabbing pain, even if he/she was shot to death.

I've also felt the love that the soul has for the person sitting in front of me as well. Sometimes it's so strong I'll say, "I'm feeling compelled to hug you right now."

Clairaudience (clear hearing)—After I sense a spirit, I'll often hear it. I might hear, "Hi, so and so! It's me, Mom!" I might hear a male or female voice, but usually it's the voice I typically hear in my head when I'm thinking ordinary thoughts. The way I know it's a soul communicating with me is that I don't usually think, "I passed away unexpectedly."

Clairvoyance (clear seeing)—Much of the communication that happens is through symbols. I'll also be shown objects and scenes from the life of the person coming through or even the person sitting in front of me. This can be tricky since a symbol may actually have up to four meanings. For example, if I see a car accident, it may mean that the person died in a car accident or that the person died accidentally.

Clairalience (Clear smelling) and Clairambience (Clear tasting)—These are the least used of my psychic senses during a reading. For example, I might smell a cigar if the soul wants me to know he was a cigar smoker.

You may have noticed that in each of the words used to describe these "psychic senses," is the word "clear." The truth is that communication from those on the Other Side may just be that simple and direct, but it's anything but "clear." The reason is that whatever is communicated has to first pass through my mind, and as I've said before, that's when the problems start.

I've tried to keep this in mind over the years, but every once in a while something happens to remind me that I'm not as smart as I think I am. For example, just a few months ago I did a session for a couple who also drove for over four hours to see me. Personally speaking, if I have to drive anywhere over two hours, I'd rather fly. So I wanted this reading to be especially good for them.

I was bringing their son through, and I kept feeling as though I was having trouble breathing. I mentioned this and stated that I felt it had something to do with their son's passing. They both nodded in agreement.

The second time I felt my throat start to constrict, I tried explaining to them why someone would commit suicide, based on what I had been told before by souls who had taken their own lives. The mother looked really distressed when I started to talk about this, so I dropped it, intending to bring it up later.

I felt myself having trouble breathing again, and once again, I started trying to explain why their son might have committed suicide. This time the mother and the father started to look distressed or I should say confused. "The part about him not being able to breathe makes sense," the mother told me, "but the part about him committing suicide doesn't make any sense at all."

"It doesn't?" I asked, stunned.

"No," the father piped in. "Our son didn't commit suicide. He drowned."

Oh my God. I could hear their son laughing at me and saying, "That's what I've been trying to tell you, but you kept cutting me off!"

I explained how I had let my own assumption as to how the

passing occurred interfere with what their son was trying to tell me. I just couldn't stop apologizing. They were gracious enough to overlook my misstep and let the reading speak for itself.

Chapter

24

Contrary to popular belief, I don't walk around all day hearing from souls and being bombarded by messages. Do spirits come to me with messages when I least expect it? It happens. When it does, I refer to those souls as "Merry Pop Ins," and sometimes they show up when I least expect it.

I was having an eye exam, and the doctor noticed an eye lash that curled into my eye. He was pulling it out with a pair of tweezers when his mother came to me. I'm assuming that she passed while he was young because she was telling me how proud she was of the man he's become and asked me to pass that message along. I told her that there was no way I was going to do that while he had tweezers a centimeter away from my eye ball!

Another time I was in a coffee shop on the Pearl Street Mall in Boulder, Colorado, when a woman who had passed from cancer asked me to pass a message to her son who was sitting at a table next to me reading a book. I chose not to.

Recently, I was in a supermarket when I had a misunderstanding with a stranger. I apologized for my part and noticed he had tears in his eyes. For the life of me I couldn't understand why. When he walked away with his young son, my lungs suddenly felt scorched. His wife died in a fire. I was at a complete loss for words. What kind of comfort could I offer him? "Excuse me, but I'm a psychic medium, and I know about your wife . . . "

I believe that when it's appropriate, the souls will bring their loved ones to me. I don't have to go looking for them. I just don't like ambushing people. There are times I will make exceptions to that rule, however . . .

I was asked to do readings at a fundraiser benefiting the Dalai Lama. When Julie, the mother of the young woman who was putting on the event heard that "someone who talked to dead people" was coming, she wasn't so sure it was a good idea. When saw me walking up to the venue, she thought, "He doesn't look evil!" Even so, she thought it might be a good idea to stay as far away from me as possible, but when souls have a message that they need to get across, sometimes they just won't be denied.

Julie was walking by me when I grabbed her arm. "Do you have a friend named Cheryl?" I asked her. She stood there looking at me with eyes wide as saucers, nodding. "You need to call her," I said. "I have her grandmother coming through, and she says that your friend's life is in danger. You need to call her now!"

Julie tried calling Cheryl, but Cheryl had changed her number and Julie didn't have her new phone number which was unlisted. So she sent Cheryl an email with "911" in the subject bar. Unfortunately, due to the circumstances that were going on in Cheryl's life at the time, she didn't have access to the Internet either, so she didn't see Julie's email for a couple of weeks.

When Cheryl finally did get back to Julie about a month later, Julie told her how she had met a guy who talked to dead people and that Cheryl's grandmother told him that her life was in danger. When Cheryl heard all of this, she was less than impressed. A guy who supposedly talked to dead people? Yeah, right. Does he talk to stop signs as well? (Well, I used to, but medication took care of that!) She did tell Julie that the day I told her this she had discovered that a gas line in her home was leaking and appeared to have been intentionally tampered with.

By the time I met Cheryl about four months later, I'd forgotten all about that warning. We hit it off, even if she did think I was off my rocker. She still wasn't a believer and remained so for about five months after we started dating. All of that changed one night when we were watching a show on television together.

I heard a voice in my head say, "Hi."

"Hi!" I responded, mentally. "Who are you?"

"My name is Shane."

Well, I didn't know anyone named Shane, so I looked at Cheryl and asked, "Did you ever know someone named Shane?"

Cheryl looked at me wide-eyed and nodded. "Why are you asking?"

I heard Shane's again. "We were high school sweethearts."

"Well, I have him coming through to me. He says he was your boyfriend in high school. Yes?"

"Yes." Cheryl was starting to look scared.

Shane began giving me more information to pass on to Cheryl so she would know it was really him. He was the high school quarterback and gregarious. She was in band, quiet and shy. He gave her his letterman jacket and a painting he had made. Cheryl acknowledged the jacket and admitted she had forgotten all about the painting.

Shane talked about how he had died. He was with Cheryl and a friend in a canoe when they lost one of the oars. Shane said he would go into the water to retrieve it. "If I don't make it, tell my mom I love her," he told Cheryl and jumped into the water.

Suddenly I felt my stomach cramping up. "He's letting me know that his stomach cramped up as soon as he jumped in the water." After I said this I expected the cramps to go away, and they did, but they came back a moment later. "He was prone to stomach cramps."

"Yes, he was," Cheryl confirmed.

"His stomach cramped, and he couldn't swim after that. He drowned." This caused Cheryl to burst into tears. "He's telling me he wasn't aware that he drowned until he saw people jumping into the water trying to find him." Cheryl told me later that his body wasn't found for several days afterwards.

"He doesn't want you to feel responsible for what happened. He's telling me you didn't even know how to swim at the time, so if you had jumped in, you would have drowned too." I didn't know this at the time, but Cheryl had broken her nose as an infant, and she never learned how to swim because she had trouble breathing out of one of her nostrils. She started weeping even harder as thirty-five years of guilt came to the surface.

"He's wants me to tell you he loves you and that there's nothing to feel guilty about."

"Please tell him I love him, and I still miss him," Cheryl said.

"You just did," I told her, and her healing began as all of her grief and guilt came rushing out in a flood of tears.

My Reading with Anthony

By Cheryl Vidakovich

I wanted to share my incredible experience of when Anthony did a reading for me. It not only healed me but also allowed me to have closure. There were a couple of reasons that this was such a powerful reading. My boyfriend had died in a boating accident in the summer of 1973, and I had no closure to his death because I didn't get a chance to say "good-bye."

After that, I shoved the memories somewhere to stop the pain and hurt I was feeling. During the reading Shane brought up memories I had buried deep in my soul so that I could begin my healing after all of these years.

In order to explain how this reading changed my life, I need to share our story with you. Shane and I were high school sweethearts. He was the well-liked, popular athlete; I was the quiet, shy, not so well-liked girl.

Shane and I were at a lake barbequing and partying with friends. Three of us—Shane, John, and I—decided to get into a rowboat and go out into the lake. We were in the middle of the lake when we decided to head back to the dock. As we were rowing back, one of the oars fell out of the boat. Being the kind of guy that Shane was, he decided to jump into the water to retrieve it. Before he jumped into the water, he took off his watch as well as his shoes and socks, all of which he handed to me along with his wallet. "If I don't make it back, tell my mom I love her," he joked. He told me he loved me, smiled and jokingly said, "Good-bye." Then he jumped into the water.

The water started to white cap whereupon John and I struggled to keep the boat from tipping. When we didn't see Shane again for several minutes and he didn't answer when we called out to him, I knew he wasn't coming back.

It took county workers five days to find Shane's body. It was five years before I would go near a lake or get into a boat.

I always had a feeling in my heart that Shane knew he would die that day. That very day he woke his mother up and took her

to church—something he had never done before, since he pre-
ferred staying home and watching sports on television. After his
passing his mother and I had many conversations about things
that Shane had done and had said that led us to believe he knew
that day would be his last.

When Anthony was doing my reading, without me asking,
Shane had told him that he knew he would die that day. He
brought up memories I had long forgotten. He talked about the
watercolor of the mountains he had painted for me. Shane talked
about his letter jackets and how he loved it when I wore them.
Both the painting and the jacket he had given me were destroyed
in a fire.

He told Anthony that he didn't realize he was dead until he
swam back to the shore of the lake and saw everyone trying
searching for him. He then mentioned the large (11″ x 14″) photo
of him at the funeral. Shane thanked me for lighting candles for
him at church. It was so comforting to hear that the candles had
meant so much to him.

Throughout the reading Shane's personality came shining
through, joking and kidding the way he always did when he was
alive. He joked about John and me letting him go into the water
knowing that he cramped so easily. I thought it would be like
Shane to joke about his death the way he was during the reading. He also discovered something positive in every situation he
found himself in.

Ever since he died, I've wondered if Shane was okay. I believed
that he was in a better place, but his death made me question my
faith and question God. Why would He take such an incredible
human being so early in his life? It just wasn't fair.

The first healing the reading brought me was hearing from
Shane that he was okay and happy. I wanted to know what
Shane's life was like now. He said that he was enjoying his life
there as much as he did when we were together here—in fact,
even more so.

More healing came when Shane said that he didn't blame me
for his death and asked me to forgive myself. "How could you

have saved me when you couldn't swim?" It's true. When I was an infant, my nose was broken and no one knew until I was older. I found out because whenever I ran or swam, I'd get horrible headaches. When I was examined by a doctor to find out why, it was discovered I could breathe out of only one of my nostrils.

The guilt I had carried for years was suddenly gone. "Please tell Shane I love him," I asked Anthony.

"You just did," he told me.

Then Anthony told me that Shane wanted me to know that he still loved me and that he always would. Even though at the time of the reading, it felt as though time had stood still and that no time had passed since his death, I can now move on with my life. I now have the closure I needed.

* * *

Chapter

25

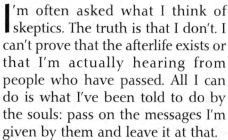

I'm often asked what I think of skeptics. The truth is that I don't. I can't prove that the afterlife exists or that I'm actually hearing from people who have passed. All I can do is what I've been told to do by the souls: pass on the messages I'm given by them and leave it at that.

It's not my responsibility to change anyone's mind as to whether communication with the soul is possible. If someone thinks that what I do is bunk and that I'm full of it, that person has the right to believe that. There have been times when I have encountered people who have thought that way right up to the time when someone they loved communicated with them from the Other Side.

Thanksgiving Day, 2007, my friend Debbie and her sister Deanna invited me to Thanksgiving dinner with them, their family, and friends. They assured me that I wouldn't have to "work" for my dinner that night, just enjoy myself.

It was a great dinner with people I knew and many I hadn't met before although I could tell by the way some of them were looking at me that they had heard about me. Despite the girl's best efforts, the conversation turned to what I do. At first, I wasn't aware that people were talking about me, but when I found out, a young man named Shane said, "No offense, but I just don't believe in what you do, and even if it were possible, there isn't anyone I'd want to talk to."

Normally, I would have let it go at that, but I didn't. It might have been the result of a combination of too much sugar and tryptophan, but I decided to "set him straight." I asked (in my head) if there were any souls who wanted to talk to Shane. Almost immediately one came through. Since I don't really remember the names of those involved in the reading other than Shane (and I had to call Debbie to find out *his* name), I'm going to make up the other names.

I looked at Shane and said, "Really? So you wouldn't want to talk to David?"

Shane looked at me stunned and asked, "Who?"

"I don't know who he is personally, but he's telling me that you do. He's telling me that you two were best friends since kindergarten. He's also telling me that he took his own life when he was eleven and you were twelve years old. He wants you to know that it's not your fault. You couldn't have stopped him from doing it. You didn't see it coming. He wants you to know that he still loves you and thinks of you as his big brother."

Shane looked at me, not saying anything.

"Oh, by the way, I have someone named Brian here too."

"I don't know who that is, "Shane said.

"Well, again, I don't know who he is either, but he says that you two were friends as well. He died when he was sixteen in a car accident. He and David want you to know that they've met and become really good buddies. They have their arms around each other's shoulders, but they don't want you to be jealous since you'll all be together again when it's your time, which, by the way, won't be anytime soon."

By this time, Shane was openly weeping. Deanna ran to him and hugged him, but he shrugged her off and ran out of the house. A couple of his friends ran out after him to comfort him.

When he finally came back into the house, an hour later, I walked up to him to ask him if he was okay, but he spent the rest of the night avoiding me, looking at me as though I had grown horns on my head.

My Reading with Anthony

By Gregory A. Raymer

I first met Anthony Quinata by chance. My first impression of him was of annoyance when he interrupted a private conversation I was having with my friend. But it was not long until I realized what was really going on: Anthony was tapped from the Other Side to give me important messages from my deceased loved ones.

I had not told anyone about my personal problems, but I was having an inner struggle from severe self-doubt and poor self-esteem issues. My mother, who knew me better than I, relayed messages of hope to Anthony, who told them to me.

At first I felt that any psychic could say general things to me, but when he mentioned events that had happened to me in my childhood that only my mother and I would have known, I knew that he was genuine. Anthony even recited quips of humor that were specific only to my mother.

Not long after, I had the epiphany that Anthony wasn't just your ordinary, everyday psychic medium; he had a true gift from God. What's more, he was only interested in the message from the Other Side. He never made up anything or only said things that the recipient wanted to hear.

His love of God and devotion to His principles further enhances his credibility with me.

I always look forward to hearing from Anthony and know that he is walking his talk.

* * *

145

Chapter

26

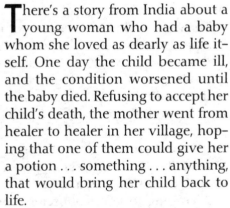

There's a story from India about a young woman who had a baby whom she loved as dearly as life itself. One day the child became ill, and the condition worsened until the baby died. Refusing to accept her child's death, the mother went from healer to healer in her village, hoping that one of them could give her a potion ... something ... anything, that would bring her child back to life.

One of the healers looked at the dead child in her arms and said, "Yes, I can make you a potion to bring this child back to life, but you must bring me something, and it will be hard to find."

"Tell me!" the mother cried. "Whatever it is, I'll get it!"

"You must bring me a rose, a single rose," the healer told her.

"That will be simple enough!" the mother said, hope rising in her heart.

"It must be a flower that comes from a house that has not experienced death."

The woman left the healer and ran to the first house she saw. "I need a rose flower to bring to a healer who will make a potion that will give my baby back to me." The people living there quickly brought her what she asked for.

She turned to run back to the healer when she remembered the condition told to her. "Have there been any deaths in your household?" she asked.

"Our parents have all died in the last five years," was the reply.

The woman ran to another house with the same request and the same condition. "I lost my husband," she was told.

From household after household she requested a rose and asked if death had come to the family. "Yes, death has touched us," she was told repeatedly.

The woman was running to another home when suddenly she stopped. She looked at her child. Her child was dead, and she realized she wasn't alone. Like so many others, she lost someone she loved. God had not singled her out. Losing someone you love and the suffering that comes from it are as common to people as a rose is to a flower garden. She returned home and began her grieving.

It's hard work to go on living when someone you love dies. One of the hardest lessons to learn is that life doesn't stop. It doesn't even slow down long enough for us to catch our breath.

According to grief counselors, there are seven stages people typically go through when they grieve. They are shock, denial, bargaining, guilt, anger, depression, and hope.

Sometimes people come to see me hoping to do what I call "The Tarzan Swing" through the stages. They seem to think that by hearing from their loved ones who have passed, they'll be able to go through the stages in one fell swoop!

It's not my job to make people feel better, only to pass on what I hear during the reading. As a medium, while I'm not an expert on grief, I do have some suggestions I'd like to make that may help you during a very difficult time.

Death is not the end of life, love, or relationships.

Try to understand that death is a doorway to a new existence, a new life—not a wall that separates you from your loved ones. Whatever you were to each other, you still are. Know that you will see your loved one again.

Talk directly to your loved ones.

This is typical dialogue that happens during a session, "[Your loved one] is saying, 'I love you.'"

"Please share my love with him/her too."

To which I'll say, "You just did."

I cannot say or stress this enough: your loved ones, even though they may not be with you physically, are still very much a part of your life. They are very much aware of what's happening in your life. They hear you when you talk to them.

Part of their journey now that they have crossed over is to help you on yours while you're still here. Take advantage of this by asking them for their guidance. They can't tell you what to do, but they can and want to support you on your journey while you're still here.

Pray for them.

Whenever I see a candle during a reading, it usually symbolizes prayers being said or prayers being asked for.

I was doing a reading for woman in which her mother came through, asking for prayers. "Why would she want me to pray for her when she's in Heaven? I would have thought she wouldn't need my prayers."

"When your mother was still here and suffering from cancer, did you pray for her?" I asked.

"Yes, I did," she answered.

"Why did you pray for her?"

"Because I loved her, and I asked God either to heal her or ease her suffering," she answered with a tear rolling down her cheek.

"Did you stop loving her when she passed away and went to be with God?"

Of course she hadn't. That's why her mother was asking for her prayers. I've been told by the souls that prayer isn't only a way of staying connected with your loved ones on the Other Side, but it's another way of saying to the souls, "I'm thinking of you and sending you love."

When I see a candle, it could also mean that the soul is asking for a candle to be lit for it. According to the souls, when you light a candle and say a prayer while you do so, as long as the flame is burning, the prayer continues being said.

I was doing a group reading when someone named Dennis came through angrily demanding to talk to a woman, I'll call Karen, who had made it clear that she didn't want to hear from him. After the session was over, she booked a private reading with me during which her grandmother came through.

Dennis kept coming to me during her session, again, angrily demanding to talk to her. "I'm sensing a lot of anger coming from him," I told her. "I'm also getting drug and alcohol abuse."

Karen nodded.

"Wow, I just heard a gunshot. Did he take his own life by shooting himself?"

"Yes," she said, but in the next breath pleaded, "Please, I really don't want to talk to him."

"I understand, but he won't leave," I told her. "He wants to talk to you."

"Well, I don't want to hear from him." When he heard this, he pulled his energy away. After her session was over, he came back and apologized to me. "I'm sorry I was being such a jerk to you, but I wanted her to know it was really me."

"I think she got that, but I don't think that she's ready to forgive you just yet," I told him.

"I'm so close to moving up to the 'next level' here," he continued. "If she'd just light a candle for me, it would really help."

I told him I'd pass that message onto her, and he left. I called her on her cell phone, but she had turned it off during her reading so my call went straight through to her voice mail. I left a message about Dennis coming to me after she had gone and what he was asking from her.

A few minutes later Dennis came back, only this time he was a different person. His energy was lighter and more loving. "Tell Karen I said, 'Thank you for the candle. It really helped. I was able to move forward thanks to her.'"

Less than a minute later I received a call from Karen, who was crying. "I just listened to your message about Dennis. Do you want to hear something crazy?"

"I'd love to," I told her.

"I was driving home, and I got this urge to get off the highway and take a right turn. It's not on my way home, but I did it anyway. I drove a couple of blocks when I saw Saint Thomas More Catholic Church. I had this overwhelming urge to light a candle for Dennis. I'm not Catholic, and I've never been in that church before, but I went in, lit a candle for Dennis, and I prayed that God help him find peace. When I came back to my car, I turned my phone back on and that's when I heard your message!"

When I told Karen that Dennis came back to me thanking her for lighting the candle, she wept even harder. "His energy felt a lot lighter," I told Karen. "It seems to me that he still has a long spiritual journey ahead of him back to God, but he's made progress thanks to you. You can continue to help him if you keep lighting candles and praying for him."

Karen thanked me and hung up. I didn't hear from her or Dennis again after that day.

Feel your feelings.

It's normal to experience feelings of emptiness, disbelief, and yearning. So is feeling stunned and dazed. Enduring moments of sheer and utter fear, confusion, shock, despair as well as feelings of being ignored, rejected, or betrayed are normal. All of these are real and natural. So is the need to express them.

During readings, when I see people not breathing, I know it's because they're trying not to cry. They're trying to control very strong emotions by keeping them inside. Don't be ashamed to cry. Crying is not a sign of weakness. To me, it's a sign of strength. It's part of healing. Tears are a sign that our bodies are rearranging the energy we're carrying. Expressing emotions is a necessary part of our being and helps you to fully come to terms with your grief.

Don't keep your grief to yourself.

It's not unusual for someone, when the reading is over, to want to tell me about the loved one who came through during the session. Talking about and sharing your sorrow is critical to moving through your grief. It also helps you adjust to life without your loved one.

Refusing to accept your loss keeps you stuck in your grief and may lead you to becoming depressed. Telling and retelling stories about your loved one and your loss will lead to acceptance. Accepting your loss, mentally and emotionally, is the first antidote for the pain you're feeling.

Seek grief counseling. Talk to a therapist. Join a bereavement group.

Seek out people who have experienced the loss of a loved one and are feeling what you feel; talking to them can be healing. Sharing your grief and reaching out for support is a proven way to handle difficult situations with major changes in your life. Talking about what you have lost, what you are missing, what you regret, what you wish you had said and done . . . will help you to accept what's happened and will give you a sense of hope that while your life may never be the same, you can move through your grief.

My Reading with Anthony

By Linda Clinger

I recently had a psychic party with psychic medium Anthony Quinata. I was amazed at how accurate he was with each of my guests. There were thirteen people in attendance who all received readings whether they were paying guests or just cynics observing.

My favorite reading that night was about a woman I have never met before who works with my daughter. Anthony described her father and then said he didn't know what this meant but the father wanted him to tell her something. He then spoke in Puerto Rican calling her the pet name he had called his daughter when she was a child. Of course this brought tears to her eyes and to others. She finally felt peace and closure knowing that he was always close by.

My father was one of the observing cynics in attendance. My mother who had passed twelve years ago had plenty to say to him. She even called him an old coot. Anyone who knew my mother knew whom Anthony was speaking of. Also my father's old friend, who had passed, came through. Anthony knew his friend's name was Joe and said that when he had passed, he owed my father money. All this was true, and Joe was my father's best man at the wedding when he married my mother.

There were many tears shed by many as they realized the reality of life after death and that our love ones remain around us. The main thing I learned from our session was that our loved ones on the Other Side continue to need our prayers.

* * *

Chapter

27

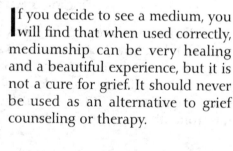

If you decide to see a medium, you will find that when used correctly, mediumship can be very healing and a beautiful experience, but it is not a cure for grief. It should never be used as an alternative to grief counseling or therapy.

Allowing Some Time to Pass

A soul can start communicating with you almost immediately after it has crossed over. Shortly after my own mother passed away, I tried to find a store open that sold candles. (Not an easy task at 2 a.m., even in Los Angeles!) My mother came to me, and said, "Hi, boy."

"Hi, Mom," I said back to her in my mind. "Are you okay?"

"I'm fine," she told me. She said that she was happy to finally "get it over with" and that she had already reunited with my father who had passed a year and a half before. We talked a little longer before she pulled her energy away, and I paid for the candle I had found for her.

I'm telling you this to illustrate a point—you can start talking to your loved ones immediately after they pass. I don't recommend, however, that you schedule an appointment with a medium immediately after you lose someone. Give yourself some time to grieve, to adjust, and to gain perspective about your loss.

How much time? I suggest that people allow at least six months, but that's only a suggestion. For you it may be more or you may need less time. Just keep in mind that the purpose of a session with a medium is not to help you get over your grief but to reassure you that your loved one has not abandoned you.

Finding a Medium

My first recommendation is that you look for the same things you would in any professional: reputation, integrity, approach, and experience. True mediums are rare, and people talk about them. If a medium is really doing what he or she claims to be doing, word of mouth travels quickly. Mediums often get referrals from other people who have seen them.

Getting the Most from Your Session

When people come to see me for a reading, they are typically nervous, somewhat skeptical, and perhaps a little afraid. I can't blame them; I would be too.

Understanding this before beginning a session, I explain how this works and how I receive information. Even though I take what I do seriously, I often inject humor to help people relax and realize that what is about to happen is not at all scary.

I'm going to share with you what I share with someone who

sees me for a session—be it private, family, phone, or small group. Here is how you can get the most out of the sitting. As the old saying goes, "Forewarned is forearmed." My hope is that after reading this, you'll be able to get the most out of your session with a medium—whether it's with me or someone else you choose to work with.

Before the Session Begins

Check your expectations at the door. It's been my experience that the best sessions happen when people come in excited about the sitting, but open to whatever happens. They may hope to hear from someone in particular, and they may hear from that person, but they flow with whatever happens.

In group sessions particularly, hoping to hear from someone specific may be disappointing because the time is limited and the person you are hoping to hear from may be "second in line." If you really are hoping to hear from someone in particular, then book a private session with a medium.

Furthermore, I believe in maintaining a "code of silence" before a session. When people come to see me, I tell them not to "talk about dead people." In other words, I don't want to know who they are hoping to reconnect with. In my opinion, this is a good practice for you to follow no matter who the medium is that you're seeing.

Keep Your Feedback to a Minimum

I've found that one of the most confusing elements of a reading for most people is how much they can say once the session starts. My answer is as little as possible. When the session begins, try to keep your answers to either "yes" or "no." Let the soul who is coming through to you do the work.

Once I was doing a session for a woman and told her, "I have a woman coming through who tells me she passed from breast cancer."

She became really excited and told me, "I know who that is! It's my mother! She had breast cancer. Her name is Charlotte!"

"I appreciate your excitement," I told her, "but from now on, try to keep your answers to 'yes' or 'no.' If this really is your mother, let's let *her* prove it to you."

Keep a Record of Your Session

Personally speaking, I don't mind if people record their session with me, but I've heard of mediums that do. I do tell people if they want to record the session, they must bring their own recorder, I don't provide the recording. I also tell them that at the very least, they should take notes. The reason for this is that some of the information that comes through to you during a session may not make sense when you hear it but may make sense later when you're not in the "hot seat."

Ask Your Questions at the End of the Session

Again, personally speaking, I don't allow questions during a session because it's been my experience that you will hear what the souls coming through need you to hear. I did this after noticing people weren't listening to what the souls were saying because they were preoccupied with questions such as, "When am I going to meet my soul mate?" or "Why did you change your will at the last minute?"

I wish I were kidding.

If you're seeing a medium who does allow you to ask questions, my suggestion would be to write them down before the session and ask them towards the end. Doing this will allow you to be present and listen to the messages you're being given.

Chapter

28

As I've mentioned before, when it comes to doing a reading for someone, I have a couple of rules. One of them is that I'm not to know who the sitter is hoping to reconnect with. If that person tells me, he's disqualified from receiving a session with me.

The second one is that if you receive a reading from me, you cannot receive another one for at least a year. I also try to discourage people from hoping to hear from the same person twice since I have no control over who will come through during a session.

When Stacy came to my home, she told me that she had seen me at an event a year and a half before. "Unfortunately, because of the size of the group you weren't able to spend much time with me, but you brought my mother through that night," she told me. "Even though you only spent a few minutes with me, I knew it was she because you had her mannerisms, and even the way she said things, down pat."

I told her that I couldn't assure her that her mother would come through again. She said that she understood. Good thing because it wasn't her mother who came through again during this particular session. The following are excerpts from the session:

"I have a male here who is making me feel that you two are close. He's hugging you and smiling at you. He's claiming to be your older brother. Does that make sense? You lost your older brother?"

Stacy nodded her head. "Yes," she said softly, as tears came to her eyes.

I couldn't believe what I was hearing next. "Oh my God, Stacy, he's telling me that you're the only one left! Is that true?"

Stacy nodded again, sobbing softly.

"He's saying he passed after your mother, who passed after your father." I told her.

"That's right. First my father passed, then my mother, and then my brother," she said softly.

"You're alone, but you're not. I say that because your brother's telling me that you're married," I continued.

"Yes, I'm married." Stacy confirmed.

"Your brother wants me to tell you to quit apologizing. He's telling me that he's the one who needs to apologize to you," I said, pointing to her, "for leaving you alone. Do you understand this?"

"Yes, but I do need to apologize to him," Stacy told me, crying even harder.

"He's motioning with his hands," I told her, mimicking what I was seeing psychically, waving my hands towards my chest. "When I see this, it means that the person is taking responsibility for his passing. Now, he's talking about alcohol. Was he an alcoholic? It feels to me as though he abused alcohol. My head is really fuzzy, and I'm feeling woozy."

"Yes, he was an alcoholic."

"He's saying that he drank himself to death."

"Yes."

"Stacy, I need to tell you that he's making me feel he wanted to die. He took your mother's passing really hard."

"He did," she agreed.

"Well, he wants you to know she was there to meet him when he crossed over. So was your father. He also wants you to know that he's okay now. He thanks you for being his 'guardian angel.' Does this make sense?"

This hit home because for the first time during the session Stacy openly wept. "I used to take care of him. When I'd take him to the hospital, he'd thank my husband for letting him 'borrow' me and he'd say that I was his 'angel.'"

"Wait a minute, he's saying that you wrote an apology letter, but it wasn't really a letter, it was an email. Does that make sense?" I asked, confused, hoping I was getting it right.

"I did! Just last night! I wrote him an email telling him how sorry I was that I wasn't there when he died."

"Well, he's telling me that you're always apologizing to him. I mean, all . . . of . . . the . . . time," I said, emphasizing the last four words.

Stacy started giggling through her tears when I told her this. "I do apologize all the time!" she said, almost embarrassed. "I keep telling myself, 'If only I had gotten to him sooner, he wouldn't have died.'"

"He wants you to know he wanted to die. There's nothing you could have done. Eventually, he would have had his way. He gave up. He wanted to be with your mother and father, and now he is. He's making peace with his life, and he wants to make peace with you."

I, too, wanted her to have some peace. "Stacy," I continued, "someday you'll be a family again. You, your husband, his family

. . . you'll all be together again."

Stacy lit up for the first time since she came to see me. "Do you really think that we'll all be together again?" she asked.

"I *know* you will," I told her. "I *promise* that you'll be together again one day. Keep praying for them until that day."

A few weeks later I received a card in the mail from Stacy.

Dear Anthony,

I'm sorry this is so late. I met with you (at your home). You made contact with my mom, brother, and briefly, with my father.

Thank you so much for sharing your gift with the world. I had been so upset at my brother's passing because I felt I should have gotten him to the hospital before he died. Your gift made me realize that he is at peace and that I would not have been able to change the outcome.

I'm still grieving my losses, but now I have peace knowing my family is together on the Other Side.

Thank you, again, for the comfort.

May God Bless You Every Day!
Stacy

If there's one thing I've learned from doing this work, and this is probably the most important lesson of all, it's that death does not end life, love, or relationships. Eventually, when it's our time, we all are reunited with those who have touched our heart and whose hearts we have touched. I promise.

Afterword

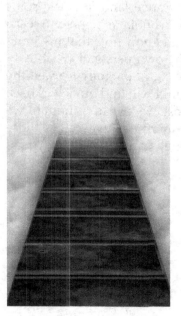

Thanksgiving Day, 2009, my mother and father were both in the hospital unit of Saint John of God's nursing facility in Los Angeles, CA. My mother was there because she broke her ankle, and my father was there after suffering a heart attack.

My sisters, Meridith and Nadine, were also there to bring them food. It wasn't as though my mom and dad weren't being fed, but my sisters brought them "island food" to eat.

Meridith went to my mother's room to get her and bring her to my father's room. Nadine went straight to my father's room. She was talking

163

to him and noticed he wasn't really paying attention to her but was looking at the ceiling off to his right.

"What are you looking at, Dad?" she asked him. "What do you see?"

Our father looked at her and said, "I've been there before, baby. I don't know when, I don't know how . . . but I've been there before."

"Where Dad, where have you been before?" Nadine asked. He didn't answer her, but kept staring into space until Meridith wheeled our mother into his room and they ate dinner.

The following morning, at 6 a.m., one of the staff found my father had crossed over.

"What do you think he saw?" Nadine asked me after telling that story.

"Home," I told her.

When it's your time, you won't be going to some strange land you've never been before. Where you'll be going, you'll be welcomed back as family.

If anything, we're strangers in a strange land *here*. The souls have repeatedly compared this life to school. We're here to learn spiritual lessons in physical existence. I know now that my journey as a medium has been part of my own personal syllabus.

When we've completed the course, and hopefully learned the lessons we came here to learn, you and I will find ourselves back home, and we'll be reunited with those we love and thought we "lost." That includes our pets, by the way. And when you see those who love you again, it'll be as though a moment hadn't pass since you last saw them.

I'll see you there.

If Tomorrow Starts without Me

When tomorrow starts without me,
And I'm not there to see,
If the sun should rise and find your eyes
All filled with tears for me,
I wish so much you wouldn't cry
The way you did today,
While thinking of the many things,
We didn't get to say.

I know how much you love me,
As much as I love you,
And each time that you think of me,
I know you'll miss me too.
But when tomorrow starts without me,
Please try to understand,
That an angel came and called my name,
And took me by the hand.

She said my place was ready,
In Heaven far above,
And that I'd have to leave behind
All those I dearly love.
But as I turned to walk away,
A tear fell from my eye
For all my life, I'd always thought,
I didn't want to die.

I had so much to live for,
So much yet to do,
It seemed almost impossible,
That I was leaving you.
I thought of all the yesterdays
The good ones and the bad,
I thought of all the love we shared,

And all the fun we had.

If I could relive yesterday
Just even for a while,
I'd say good–bye and kiss you
And maybe see you smile.
But then I fully realized,
That this could never be;
For emptiness and memories
Would take the place of me.

And when I thought of worldly things,
I might miss come tomorrow,
I thought of you, and when I did,
My heart was filled with sorrow.
But when I walked through heaven's gates,
I felt so much at home;
When God looked down and smiled at me,
From His great golden throne.

He said, "This is eternity,
And all I've promised you.
Today your life on earth is past,
But here it all starts anew.
I promise no tomorrow,
But today will always last;
And since each day's the same day,
There's no longing for the past.
You have been so faithful,
So trusting and so true;
Though there were times
You did some things
You knew you shouldn't do.
But you have been forgiven
And now at last you're free;
So won't you come and take my hand

And share my life with me?"

So when tomorrow starts without me,
Don't think we're far apart,
For every time you think of me,
I'm right here in your heart.

Attributed to David M. Romano

About the Author

Anthony Quinata was born on Guam, a tiny island in the South Pacific. Both of his parents were also from Guam, but with a father serving in the US Navy, his family frequently moved around the world and throughout the US as Anthony was growing up. Anthony's fascination and passion for all things paranormal began in childhood while listening to family ghost stories. He eventually became a paranormal investigator, specializing in hauntings, apparitions, and poltergeist activity. It was during this time that he discovered and developed his latent talents and began to embrace his work as a psychic medium, which has continued now for more than fifteen years.

There is now no doubt that Anthony is a gifted medium whose work never fails to touch and help others. He is also a spiritual teacher and author. You can learn more about Anthony at his Web site: www.AnthonyQuinata.com.

4TH DIMENSION PRESS

An Imprint of A.R.E. Press

4th Dimension Press is an imprint of A.R.E. Press, the publishing division of Edgar Cayce's Association for Research and Enlightenment (A.R.E.).

We publish books, DVDs, and CDs in the fields of intuition, psychic abilities, ancient mysteries, philosophy, comparative religious studies, personal and spiritual development, and holistic health.

For more information, or to receive a catalog, contact us by mail, phone, or online at:

4th Dimension Press
215 67th Street
Virginia Beach, VA 23451-2061
800-333-4499

4THDIMENSIONPRESS.COM

EDGAR CAYCE'S A.R.E.

Who Was Edgar Cayce?
Twentieth Century Psychic and Medical Clairvoyant

Edgar Cayce (pronounced Kay-Cee, 1877-1945) has been called the "sleeping prophet," the "father of holistic medicine," and the most-documented psychic of the 20th century. For more than 40 years of his adult life, Cayce gave psychic "readings" to thousands of seekers while in an unconscious state, diagnosing illnesses and revealing lives lived in the past and prophecies yet to come. But who, exactly, was Edgar Cayce?

Cayce was born on a farm in Hopkinsville, Kentucky, in 1877, and his psychic abilities began to appear as early as his childhood. He was able to see and talk to his late grandfather's spirit, and often played with "imaginary friends" whom he said were spirits on the other side. He also displayed an uncanny ability to memorize the pages of a book simply by sleeping on it. These gifts labeled the young Cayce as strange, but all Cayce really wanted was to help others, especially children.

Later in life, Cayce would find that he had the ability to put himself into a sleep-like state by lying down on a couch, closing his eyes, and folding his hands over his stomach. In this state of relaxation and meditation, he was able to place his mind in contact with all time and space—the universal consciousness, also known as the super-conscious mind. From there, he could respond to questions as broad as, "What are the secrets of the universe?" and "What is my purpose in life?" to as specific as, "What can I do to help my arthritis?" and "How were the pyramids of Egypt built?" His responses to these questions came to be called "readings," and their insights offer practical help and advice to individuals even today.

The majority of Edgar Cayce's readings deal with holistic health and the treatment of illness. Yet, although best known for this material, the sleeping Cayce did not seem to be limited to concerns about the physical body. In fact, in their entirety, the readings discuss an astonishing 10,000 different topics. This vast array of subject matter can be narrowed down into a smaller group of topics that, when compiled together, deal with the following five categories: (1) Health-Related Information; (2) Philosophy and Reincarnation; (3) Dreams and Dream Interpretation; (4) ESP and Psychic Phenomena; and (5) Spiritual Growth, Meditation, and Prayer.

Learn more at EdgarCayce.org.

What Is A.R.E.?

Edgar Cayce founded the non-profit Association for Research and Enlightenment (A.R.E.) in 1931, to explore spirituality, holistic health, intuition, dream interpretation, psychic development, reincarnation, and ancient mysteries—all subjects that frequently came up in the more than 14,000 documented psychic readings given by Cayce.

The Mission of the A.R.E. is to help people transform their lives for the better, through research, education, and application of core concepts found in the Edgar Cayce readings and kindred materials that seek to manifest the love of God and all people and promote the purposefulness of life, the oneness of God, the spiritual nature of humankind, and the connection of body, mind, and spirit.

With an international headquarters in Virginia Beach, Va., a regional headquarters in Houston, regional representatives throughout the U.S., Edgar Cayce Centers in more than thirty countries, and individual members in more than seventy countries, the A.R.E. community is a global network of individuals.

A.R.E. conferences, international tours, camps for children and adults, regional activities, and study groups allow like-minded people to gather for educational and fellowship opportunities worldwide.

A.R.E. offers membership benefits and services that include a quarterly body-mind-spirit member magazine, *Venture Inward*, a member newsletter covering the major topics of the readings, and access to the entire set of readings in an exclusive online database.

Learn more at EdgarCayce.org.

EDGARCAYCE.ORG